TABLE OF CONTENTS

3

Introduction

As a little boy growing up in the 1960s I remember playing with my Marx Toy Company "Ft. Apache" play set, creating all types of battle scenarios where the cavalry rode in and saved the day. The action figure Indians fell left and right as my heroes came to the rescue. Somewhat enigmatically, I always chose the most noble-looking Indian figure as a scout assisting the cavalry to defeat, and slaughter, the more fearsome looking warriors. Everyday after school, or on weekends, the good guys were victorious. Despite indigenous roots from Mexican-born grandmothers, and the incorporating of good Indians assisting the cavalry victories, the likelihood of complete Indian victories over the soldiers never crossed my mind.[1] It was common for me to entertain my elementary school friends with stories of visiting family in Mexico and engaging in perilous battles with savage Indians swooping down from the mountains to harass local farmers (I had a really vivid imagination!).

My childhood fantasies were filled with dramatic images of bloodthirsty Indians bent on terrorizing civilized families, yet my real experience with Indians was limited to passing exchanges with Tarahumara vendors selling their wares; or dancing, in the plazas of southern Chihuahua towns. Dressed in their traditional garb the distrustful Natives left a minimal impression on me; they lacked the feathers, tomahawks and war paint of "real Indians." It was not until my teens when I began to distinguish between my fantasy Indians and real Natives. A family connection to the New Mexico horseracing circuit took me to Ruidoso Downs, and the nearby Mescalero Apache Reservation, which over the years led to friendships with local residents. Many of the archaic images of the savage Indian were soon supplanted with behaviors and traditions of people not too different from those of my own family.

Those teen years gave me the small window of opportunity to crawl out of the murky shadows of cultural ignorance. To a substantial degree I had failed to acknowledge the indigenous Tarahumara roots so prevalent in my own family traditions. I will not necessarily identify this shift as an epiphany, although there has been significant acceptance of an indigenous identity influencing my life, and especially career. Symptomatic of this problem, however, I realize I could have functioned just as successfully (perhaps not as a Native American historian) in today's society had I maintained those fallacious childhood images of Indians. I was fortuitous enough to experience indigenous families in contemporary settings as genuine people, rather than the "Indian," mythological American representation, I had grown up with: I had begun to break away from the mainstream. I no longer could accept the racialized and culturally insensitive depiction of Natives that mainstream America incorporated into the nation's master narrative.

In retrospect, I ask myself how I ever believed those false Indian images of my childhood. My answer to myself is: film and television. Raised in a generation benefiting from 1950s re-runs, 1960s contemporary series, and afternoon and late-night feature film cinema programming which included films from the 1940s and '50s, I was inundated with a plethora of western iconography espousing the tradition of westward expansion, an indefatigable pioneer spirit overcoming nature's incessant obstacles to progress; in particular, the Indian. Whether it was John Wayne, Guy Madison, or Audie Murphy, in such places as the Dakota Territory, along the Oregon Trail, or the Arizona desert, the virtuous and civilized American, with his superior morals and modern technology, claimed the wilderness in the name of progress. The characters, locations, and sub-plots changed, but the universal trope remained the same: god-fearing, civilized American man will defeat nature's heathen, savage Indian.

A few years back I submitted an article for review to the UCLA Native American Center dealing with the same subject matter as this work, needless to say, it was rejected. "It's been done before, tell me something new" was the one criticism that haunted me for months. The rejection was bad enough, but to insinuate that I was rehashing old material really bothered me. The more I thought about this comment the more I became upset at myself for not getting my point out sufficiently for the reader. The study of Native American portrayals in film has been done before. There is no debating this. What I argue is that these studies focused on elements failing to recognize the importance race has played in constructing the national conscience through the portrayal of these images.

More importantly, over the course of three hundred years of popular culture; civic organizations, literature, novels, plays, and film the colonizer language employed to justify the exploitation of Natives has survived the test of time to become a non-contested element in the national conscience. Through decades upon decades of language and images depicting people of color in less than flattering perceptions most Americans are unaware they still harbor racialized attitudes about non-Whites. Scholars and intellectuals are not immune to this ideological malady.

The social problems that afflict certain groups can be explained through theories concocted through years of education, research and personal experiences, but our own *weltanschauung* continues to interfere with the ability to understand the problems of societies and cultures atypical of our own. Therefore my point, while it is true that the criticism of Native Americans in film has experienced its share of studies, like the American culture these scholars come from, they are unaware of amalgamation of ideas and beliefs on race that prevent them from understanding the powerful significance race plays in the study of Native American contemporary themes.

Thus the critics statement, "so, tell me something new!" becomes the crux in understanding the White (sub)Conscience. Although well intentioned, over the course of the past three decades scholars have been examining and criticizing film depictions of Indians quite thoroughly. Educated and well-informed contemporary scholars have exposed traditional historian's misleading portrayal of Native Americans in United States history during the past two centuries. But did they really understand the problem? And if my argument is to be fully understood in its proper context, we need to start at the field's genesis to appreciate the flaws those previous studies contained in their analysis.

Beginning with the early studies of Ralph and Natasha Friar's *The Only Good Indian* (1972), Gretchen Bataille and Charles Silet's *Pretend Indians* (1980); to more recent works such as, Michael Hilger's *From Savage to Nobleman* (1995), Ward Churchill's *Fantasies of the Master Race* (1998), Jacquelyn Kilpatrick's *Celluloid Indians* (1999) and Beverly Singer's *Wiping the War Paint Off the Lens* (2001); each offers sound examinations of Indians in cinema. Although these critical landmark studies offer outstanding analysis of Native American film representations and Hollywood's sordid record relative to this issue, I feel there is a need to understand the industry's reasons for depicting those images and audiences' failure to recognize any insensitive portrayal of Natives. This behavior is a result of the institutionalization of America's racist legacy within a subliminal ideology identified as the White (sub)Conscience.

Rooted in a colonizer mentality devised over centuries of colonial oppression to defend Northern (White) Europe's exploitation of people of color. In the

8

light of post-WWII global struggles for human rights and self-determination the open defense of colonialism became untenable, at best. Whether planned or by chance, new strategies of racial oppression developed supplanting the overt racist colonizer ideology with language critical of the old system while maintaining the privilege of power gained during colonialism. A Shadow ideology sustaining a construct of White racial superiority veiled in the rhetoric of a social conscience supporting contemporary concepts of social and racial equality. However, nearly four hundred years of propaganda tools, the White political, social and economic hegemony over Natives the 180 degree ideological transformation fully repudiating the offensive perception of non-Whites is difficult at best. The economic and social privileges gained as a result of colonialist doctrine have proven too difficult to sacrifice in the name of civil rights. The panacea of what I call the White (sub)Conscience provides Americans with the rationalization to deny any continued oppression of people of color through the talk of equality, while internally holding on to the negative perceptions of non-Whites inherited from previous generations. Specifically the vulgar representation this country generated of Native Americans during the westward movement of the eighteenth and nineteenth centuries.

Within an era of "multiculturalism" and "diversity" the White (sub)Conscience defends anachronistic racist and demeaning images of Natives, while identifying the People as dependent on White paternalistic guidance. A generation of young Americans consumed these images as part of their Saturday afternoon, or late-night television diet. These representations helped engender the subliminal ideology that convinced Americans of their altruistic view of Natives, while in fact sustaining the racist, colonizer images of Natives that soothed the national conscience as government and corporate entities battled to obtain control of Native resources at the People's detriment.

9

The historical development of this ideology is a critical factor in understanding contemporary America's inability to comprehend its delusional concept of multiculturalism and diversity. Film and television helped nurture a generation of children to accept the unquestioned imagery of Natives, contemporary Americans maintain still today as authentic depictions of their "Indians." The first series of studies conducted during the 1970s, '80s ushered in a debate over "Indian" imagery in film, and Native roles in the industry. The door has been opened. A more advanced level of historical analysis is necessary to build on the arguments those seminal studies on Natives and film has set in motion.

The focus of these works might be considered redundant, if not for the differing creative interpretation each generation of studies engenders. Although the works re-examine many of the same films, the level of analysis of these studies adds a new dimension to the ever-growing field. The earlier works set the foundation for the criticism of Indians in film. Two key components of these studies are Hollywood's misrepresentation of Natives on screen and the industry's failure to employ more Natives as actors. As these issues dominate the arguments in these works, less time is spared to discuss the effects of the images themselves on the mainstream conscience.

It was the Friar's 1972 seminal study, *The Only Good Indian*, that first examined Hollywood's inconsistent and distorted image of Natives in film. Researching thousands of silent film era and sound period movies, the Friars exposed a Hollywood tradition that sought to homogenize Indian images into a more easily defined, and recognized, character; the commodified Indian that mainstream American easily identified as other. The Friars also brought attention to various filmmaking issues affecting Native Americans, including the steady decline of Natives in cinema, the use of highly racist stories as screenplays, and "the

10

hypocrisy of all film-makers who try to justify the making of Indian films on behalf of the Native American."[2] The Friars planned to rescue the Natives from Hollywood's icon depository.

The Friar's primary concern was identifying Hollywood's callous disregard for Native American culture as a feature of the industry, even as it was producing films replete with Indian images, albeit with few actual Natives. Beginning with 17th and 18th century escape narratives, and the subsequent 19th century theater, romance novels and dime novel literature, the Friars developed the evolution of Indian imagery as part of the American entertainment mechanism. Over the course of the nation's history the Indian image acquired a general social meaning that was based more on Anglo-American concepts of "Indian-ness," and less on those of a Native social construct. The cinematic Indian contained the features and behavior the American national psyche considered the norm for three hundred years. Whether as noble savage, or bloodthirsty heathen, the iconic Indian became a critical component in the American social dialogue; the Friars exposed Hollywood's misuse of the Native within this context.

The Friars detailed analysis of the cinematic Indian set the standard by which later works of its kind must be compared. Their study is to be lauded for its visionary attack on Hollywood's exploitative use of Indians, and the industry's failure to recognize Native Americans as a distinct set of peoples, with diverse customs and beliefs. The Indian had become the exclusive property of the American media apparatus, with Hollywood (and as the Friars point out, European filmmakers also) as the authoritative consultants of "Indian-ness."

As the Friars so efficiently explain, these Indian images became more and more the assets of Hollywood. Native American authenticity was eliminated in the name of "Indian" realism. Thus, as Hollywood maintained the national Indian icon in its western screenplays, it gradually removed Natives from the screen in order to depict more natural looking Indian images; characters authentic according to Hollywood standards. The Friars pointed out the large number of Native actors present in early American cinematic features of the 1910s and '20s, and although the stories maintained the national image of Indians, during the era Native actors were able to make a living playing their Hollywood doppelganger. For convenience's sake and studio typecasting beliefs that Indians were "too stoic" and "unemotional" to act out parts, non-Native actors replaced Natives on screen, thus depriving the latter of acting opportunities. Other than John Ford's troupe-like use of Navajos as all-purpose Indians, few Natives found work in Hollywood, even as lead Indian characters.

By 1972, the publishing date of *The Only Good Indian*, Hollywood began to claim a change in its strategy of the characterization of Indians. A more sympathetic and culturally accurate image became the industry's goal. Here the Friars succeeded in exposing Hollywood's flawed commitment to accuracy. Citing critical errors in cultural accuracies in contemporary films in the early-1970s, most notably the depiction of a Mandan ritual as a Lakota practice in *A Man Called Horse (1970)*, the Friars sustain a steady attack upon Hollywood's treatment of Indians. Yet, even in this critically acclaimed and highly respected work, the Friars fail to explain the social implications the continued use of these images has on Americans.

Although *The Only Good Indian* does suggest strong racialized, if not, out and out racist, ideology affecting the development of the Hollywood Indian, it fails to explain how the continued use of these images has a direct correlation to the national social conscience's need to excuse its treatment of people of color, in this case, Native Americans. In the chapter "Welcome To Vespucci Land" the Friar's poignant use of "They came in the name of..." assails the colonizer-fueled motives to identify the European rationale for

12

exploitation of Native Americans. As the Friars argue, "Each succeeding wave of whites wrote a new scene in the tragedy. Attempts were continually made to subjugate, contain, reform, assimilate, divide, remove, and exterminate the Native American."[3] But documenting the historical results of American behavior towards Natives is only half the task; there are far deeper issues that require a separate, but equally significant, examination of how the behaviors of Anglo-Americans towards people of color, in this case Native Americans, remain largely unchanged over the nation's history.

In 1980 Gretchen Bataille and Charles Silet co-edited the highly regarded *The Pretend Indians: Images of the Native Americans in the Movies*, a work adding considerable legitimacy to the arguments extensively discussed by the Friars in 1972. *Pretend Indians* consists of a collection of previously published 1970s era works criticizing the film industry for its failed use of Indians within the industry, as actors advisors, and, most importantly, in the film portrayals. Lakota scholar Vine Deloria gives an impressive foreword that suggests a critical component of Indian imagery most Native American scholars reiterate in their works; the concept of an "American Fantasy." Deloria writes of the colonizer tool designed by white Americans to deflect the charges of the white supremacist colonialism's exploitation of Natives. Thus, in using the Indian image in literature and film American society continues to stagger under its ceaseless attempts to re-write history to legitimize its hegemonic control over the continent, its indigenous inhabitants, and most importantly, its vast supply of natural resources.

In the foreword Deloria established the tone the contributing writers will employ: "Underneath all the conflicting images of the Indian one fundamental truth emerges—the white man *knows* (Deloria's emphasis) that he is an alien and he *knows* that North America is Indian—and he will never let go of the Indian image because he thinks that by some clever manipulation he

13

can achieve an authenticity that cannot ever be his."[4] Although the majority of the articles suggest some form of a colonizer mentality, the works fail to link behavior to the gradual development of the subliminal, and often overt, racist conscience America uses to understand indigenous people.

What I suggest is that these critiques, rather than exploring a correlation to the existence of a racist agenda fueling Hollywood's misappropriated use of Indians, or explaining the continued survival of the practice during the past few centuries, are only organized into thematic sections that limit the essays to criticisms of actions, rather than content.[5] The criticisms of Hollywood's actions towards Natives is directly related, and persistently ignored, to the social context influencing studio activity, then and now. This is America's White (sub)Conscience at work.

Rita Keshena's criticism of Jewish director Ted Kotcheff's handling of his failure to employ an Indian as a consultant for his western, filmed on location in Israel, *Billy Two Hats*, is an example of the admission of an Indian image problem without developing the social milieu affecting the decision-making behind the actions. In her article Keshena focuses on Kotcheff's brushing aside criticism for his use of a generic Indian time, place, and characters in his film. He defends his actions by explaining that he had hired Indians as extras, thus he could turn to them for advice. Keshena further claims that, in an interview, Kotcheff became angry and defensive when a reporter broached his decision to him.

The director launched into a tirade declaring a long list of social causes he had been involved in. He further insisted, "that in this film injustice would be presented as universal in its application, since there are, in actuality, no ethnic differences in people, there is only the shared human experience."[6] It is doubtful that a person, such as Kotcheff, with a religious historical background that includes the anti-Semitic Spanish Inquisition, eastern European pogroms, and Nazi

14

Germany's Holocaust would accept the depiction of any of those events as generic "human" characterizations. Likewise, there is nothing generic about the genocide inflicted upon Native Americans during the past five hundred years. This is the real injustice of Kotcheff's behavior. The beneficiary of the economic windfall of cinema's capitalistic nature, Kotcheff was unable to see through his colonizer eyes his own contribution to the oppression of Native Americans. Kotcheff acts in a racist manner, yet America's racialized image of Natives prevents him from recognizing his behavior as such.

Just as important as Kotcheff's contradictory argument for his Indian depictions is Keshena's inability to understand the director's racialized comments. How does Keshena fail to see the irony between Kotcheff's Jewish personal history and his complete and utter disregard for the historical circumstances of Native Americans? Keshena's deficiency stems from her failure to identify the influence race has, even on those people subjected to the most horrible acts of brutality themselves.

Further exacerbating the nation's Indian identity problem are works such as those of the movie historian Richard Schickel. Distinguished as the creator of the 1973 television series, "The Men Who Made The Movies," and the 1976 follow up "Life Goes to the Movies," (1976), and Clint Eastwood's biographer. Richard Schickel offered his own criticism of Hollywood's depiction of Indians: needless to say, it was a less than favorable commentary towards the studio's shifting view of a more complex depiction of Indian/white relations. The most disturbing issue in the article was Schickel's nostalgic plea for a time when Americans did not have to deal with the complicated Indian images contemporary 1970s filmmakers were depicting. In his article, "Why Indians Can't Be Villains Any More," first published in *The New York Times* in 1975, Schickel complains that films such as, *Little Big Man* (1970) and *Soldier Blue (1970)* create images of

15

Indians that are too confusing to the viewer. Depicting scenes where Americans commit atrocities against Indians suggest that whites "...have been, since the beginning of time, in every clime, genocidal in our racism."[7] The portrayal of Indians as victims of Anglo-American atrocities goes beyond Schickel's concept of realism.

Schickel lauds Robert Aldrich's *Ulzana's Raid* (1972) for the accurate use of landscape, costumes, and most importantly, the storyline of a savage Indian murder spree to retell the story of the American frontier.[8] His idea of legitimate filmmaking involved the continued depiction of Indians as heartless, savage beasts. If Americans are to understand the settlement of the frontier, Schickel suggests, belligerent Indians threatening American settlers is the proper direction to take. He does not consider exploitative eastern-owned and funded corporations, land speculators, railroad monopolies, pro-industry federal policies or Anglo settler's general abhorrence of Mexicans, Chinese, Blacks, or Indians as part of the frontier narrative.

If whites did in fact victimize Indians, Schickel implies, society should move forward. "I don't wish to be held responsible for whatever crimes the white man committed in the course of that ancient, extended guerrilla conflict any more than Indians want to be held responsible for his (sic) ancestor's depredations."[9] Schickel would have a point, if his characterization was true. Over the past half-century scholars have proven once and for all that the frontier wars were generally one-sided affairs instigated by Americans (English during the colonial era) to further economic ambitions. The few incidents where Natives were victorious have been duly identified as "massacres," per the colonizer language employed by defenders of the American continental war of conquest. Thus, Schickel can justify his sentiments, and long for an era when straightforward and accurate depictions of settlers, not Indians, uphold the virtues of a white supremacist America. The failure to place his views in the proper context of the perpetuation of racist thought stimulated by a colonizer mentality are at the root his wish for the continued depiction of Indians in such demeaning images. During the 1980s few works examined Hollywood's use of Indians beyond the initial lines of reasoning of the Friars and the Bataille and Silet efforts. In 1986 Michael Hilger released *The American Indian in Film*, a decade-by-decade analysis of Indian stereotypes in films, followed by a short synopsis of films containing Indian images. In 1995 Hilger updated the work, re-titling the newer version, *From Savages to Nobleman: Images of Native Americans in Film*. The most significant feature in both of Hilger's studies is his extensive thumbnail sketch analysis of Indian films. Obviously spending countless hours analyzing a plethora of Indian films, breaking-down plots, and determining whether Indian characters functioned as noble or savage stereotypes, Hilger's work is a superb undergraduate text for a course in Native Americans in cinema. He provides the reader with a sound background on Native Americans in film and, even if his examination of the issues plaguing the film industry's depiction, and use, of Indians is not developed in depth, it is quite well done.

Like most undergraduate texts, Hilger's two works focus on gathering general information and concepts that provide the reader with basic knowledge of the material. The developing of ideas and concepts occurs in upper-division and graduate level instruction; undergraduate learning causes the student to experience a variety of disciplines at a superficial degree. This is Hilger's flaw. His analysis of Indian imagery in film is developed only to a level that informs the reader that a problem exists with Indians in Hollywood. An example of his superficial analysis of cinematic Indian imagery is his criticism of Hollywood's "side-kick Indian" stereotype, which describes how, "...techniques of composition, especially placement of characters in the frame, often favor the white hero by placing him more in the foreground and higher in the frame than with other characters." "Such placement," he continues, "is typical in films with Native Americans who are companions of the hero."[10]

Although Hilger has made a coherent academic observation, and uses recognized serials and films to develop his examples of this practice quite thoroughly, he fails to explain the social and cultural ideologies afflicting the nation that perpetuate these cinematic traditions. This kind of analysis is symptomatic of a thinking process developed in a society determined to see cultural flaws only to the point where blame can be rationalized away. Anglo-Americans' justifiable guilt is veiled through layers of social archetypes popular culture employs in its sacrosanct cant to the masses, while scholars aid the cause by using culturally acceptable theories that distract society away from real insight.

While Hilger's marginal anti-colonial analysis exposes itself to criticism, Ward Churchill's *Fantasies of the Master Race: Literature, Cinema and the Colonization of American Indians* (1998) proves more problematic. While it is well known that the controversial Churchill's research has come under serious scrutiny recently, one can not deny his Jihad-like criticism of America's abuse of Native rights, thus his analysis proves even more enigmatic. As the subtitle indicates, Churchill examines both cinema and the colonization of Native Americans, thus one expects this fine study to address the critical features of Indian imagery in film and Hollywood's role in maintaining a colonial stranglehold over Indians. Yet, even Churchill fails to develop the concepts of colonialism and race fully beyond his insightful commentary. First published in 1992 as a compilation of previously published articles, the updated version remains theoretically faithful to its predecessor, "...exploring the ways in which literature and its celluloid stepchild, the cinema, have employed in combination with supposedly nonfiction venues to falsify the realities of Euroamerica's interaction with the continent's indigenous peoples." Churchill defines the book's purpose as, "to strip away at least some of the elaborate veil of misimpression and disinformation behind which the ugly countenance of Euroamerican conquest, colonization and genocide have been so carefully hidden."[11]

Much of Churchill's effort satisfactorily accomplishes the theoretical goal set forth above. Churchill's works persuasively expose the colonialist construct prevalent in literary and cinematic works considered academic and/or commercial successes. Although his essays astutely rebuke scholars and filmmakers for a persistent behavior that evokes colonialist concepts, still Churchill underestimates the value of a White (sub)Conscience in its role of defending colonialism.

In different forms, under assorted social or academic identities the basic principles associated with colonialism, repression and exploitation, continue to thrive. This happens because the racist context of colonialism has been incorporated into the nation's (perhaps, even global) social sub-consciousness. Churchill's two essays critical of the theoretical arguments expressed in the works of James Clifton and Werner Sollors, that examine culture and ethnicity, typify this problem.

Churchill believes that the theoretical conclusions expressed in Clifton's *The Invented Indian* (1990) and Sollors' *Beyond Ethnicity* (1986) are the views of extremist hate-mongers whose baseless findings are the result of unsound research, or personal vendettas against Native Americans. Churchill expresses his distaste for the contributors to Clifton's work by claiming that the most encouraging result from the release of *The Invented Indian*, "… lies in the open self-identification of a whole cast of North American neonazis."[12] And as for Sollors, Churchill is upset because Sollors concept of ethnicity is too "WASPish."[13]

Churchill feels Sollors seeks to "manipulate into apparent existence a circumstance wherein everyone—white and non-white alike—fits into what Sollors wishes to project as a single, holistic 'American' socio-cultural matrix based upon a mutuality of consent among all concerned."[14] For Sollors ethnic identity becomes subordinate to a singular national identity.

In the defense of *The Invented Indian*, it is relatively safe to say neither the editor nor the contributing writers are neo-nazis. As for Sollors "WASP" interpretation of ethnicity, according to Churchill, Sollors is himself of WASP descent, therefore Churchill should not be surprised that Sollors views on ethnicity are skewed away from a colored, more specifically Native American, understanding. The problem with the two works is not the conclusions that demean Natives, or seek to homogenize ethnicity. The sticking points with Clifton and Sollors, and overlooked by Churchill, are the social and cultural ideologies propagating such white supremacist principles. Condemning these works as academically unsound appear as the ramblings of a demented radical to the academic core Churchill is attacking. Criticizing Clifton and Sollors for expressing ideas that are contrary to the welfare of Natives is tantamount to accusing the Klan of being the cause of the repression of blacks in the post-Civil War South. A major criticism scholars have about pro-Indian film depictions of two notorious exterminators of Native Americans, George Custer and John Chivington, is that they are portrayed as lunatics, out of touch with reality, and therefore not representative of mainstream American attitudes about Natives. Yet history has proven anti-Indian sentiments to have dominated nineteenth century discourse. It is the social conscience of America that needs a strong tongue-lashing from Churchill, not Clifton's essayists or Sollors; they are mere bit-players in the larger battle of American (white) social, political, and economic hegemony over non-whites.

Although astutely aware of colonizer behavior, its social and economic effects, and the role literature and cinema in this drama, Churchill still limits his argument by criticizing only individuals, or individual works, and by not placing his ideas in the larger proper social context. Colonizer literature and cinema exist because Americans are comfortable with their soothing message of social and cultural (and religious, for that matter) righteousness. A symbiotic relationship exists where the arts and media protect, inform, and reflect the public on issues of existing racial beliefs. Concepts descended from eras of racial intolerance aid in institutionalizing the ideas to the point that the most learned academician perversely accepts these social ideas on race and people of color as unbiased and non-judgmental. It is not surprising that film and television producers, directors, and writers are afflicted by the same contagion.

It is not enough to identify the effects of colonialism, or the manner in which a novelist, screenwriter, or a scholar expresses colonialist philosophy. The mere denunciation of colonialism only partially exposes the malevolence of this repressive system. The White (sub)Conscience is a social ideology that reduces colonialism to an antiquated tool of imperialism. It then further diminishes colonialism as a theoretical explanation of social and economic inequalities. It never answers why the inequalities persist. Within intellectual discourse, the White (sub)Conscience reduces theoretical constructs of anti-colonialist and race theory to mere rhetoric. The discourse simply disguises the root of all oppression; colonialism becomes neo-colonialism, which is then supplanted by industrial globalization, which, in turn, leads to wars against terrorism that contribute to invasions of nations to remove putative weapons of mass destruction.

The persistence of the White (sub)Conscience provides Americans the ideological mechanism to

21

maintain its intimidating relationship with people of color. Like its foreign targets, within the U.S. borders, this principle manifests itself in the racialized depiction of dependent and helpless Natives advocating government and corporate America's management of the People and their resources.

In the decade following Churchill's first publication of *Fantasies of the Master Race* in 1992 outstanding works on Native Americans and film have been published. Many continue to focus on the negative stereotyping of Natives in film and television and further develop concepts first introduced by the works of Ralph and Natasha Friar and Gretchen Bataille and Charles Silet. A critical shift occurring during the 1990s has been the increase in Native American scholars examining this issue, most notably the aforementioned Churchill, and recently Jacquelyn Kilpatrick and Beverly Singer.

To their credit, Kilpatrick and Singer add a dimension to their work affirming that positive change for Native Americans has occurred within the film industry. Both Kilpatrick and Singer do the obligatory denouncement of Indian imagery in film, but each examines contemporary issues that earlier critics overlooked, or had yet to develop. Kilpatrick admirably re-examines the customary pre-1970s genre westerns and the social issues influencing scripts and stereotypes. However, it is her analysis of more recent films (1970s-1990s) that raises her study to a higher degree.

Beginning with *Tell Them Willie Boy is Here* (1969), to *A Man Called Horse* (1970), on through the blockbuster film *Dances With Wolves* (1990), to lesser-known films such as *War Party* (1988) and *Sunchaser* (1996), Kilpatrick resumes the criticism of the seemingly never-ending inaccuracies Hollywood steadfastly harbors in its works. She also emphasizes the role Native actors played, as early as the silent era, in combating many of the Hollywood stereotypes. However, the most compelling feature of her work is the critique of films produced and written by Native Americans.

Like Kilpatrick, Singer also examines Native American cinema, although she focuses on independent projects, while Kilpatrick focuses on Hollywood sponsored features. Both scholars help introduce an element of Native American creative expression long overlooked by scholars. It is works such as these that place Native Americans in the context as active participants, rather than as oppressed and powerless victims. It is a significant leap forward in the manner Native Americans and cinema have been examined. At the same time, many of the issues Kilpatrick and Singer examine early in their works; regardless their contemporary interpretations, remain constrained by academic traditions. Although theoretically sound, these works lack the most important dimensional feature that binds the behavior of Americans towards people of color, specifically Natives, and the nation's subliminal mind.

The American subliminal consciousness has been bombarded so frequently with the justifications for colonial oppression, and the racial bigotry associated with colonialism, that Americans take for granted any biased attitudes related to marginalized people. The reason certain people fail to succeed in America, the consensus argument will suggest, is that they are unable to adapt or keep up with "progress." It is this "progress," a euphemism for capitalism, which motivates the nation to engage in a two century old strategy of protecting the rights of a European-origins white community to exploit this economic system to its most efficient level. Unfortunately for those people not considered part of the inner circle of progress, the most efficient economic exploitation of resources in a capitalist system requires the development of a social class of people who are denied the opportunities to participate in the wealth accumulation competition, but who are absolutely central to the situation as workers.

The Nigerian-born poet Chinweizu has argued that there is a direct correlation between the maturity of industrialization that European states reached during the nineteenth century and the extent of their colonialist holdings, with the British Empire setting the standard of development in the economically related institutions.[15] Possessors of an almost endless supply of natural resources from their African, Asian, or Latin American holdings, European states transformed themselves into nascent industrialist powers. Rather than confronting their rapacious behavior, the Europeans sought to defend themselves by creating a colonizer mentality that placed the blame for the depressed conditions of people of color (colonized) on the Natives themselves.

The Martinique anti-colonialist writer, Frantz Fanon, explains the one fundamental principle associated with colonialism is that the colonialist (the settler) refuses to accept responsibilities for his/her acts against the colonized (Natives). But the reason the Europeans must venture to far off exotic lands is due to a shortage of resources in the homeland. Their colonizing adventures are related to a dearth of materials to feed the ravenous appetite of industrialization.

Endowed with an overabundance of land, and in fact suffering a labor shortage, the scholars will argue, the United States does not fall under the same category of the European colonialists who raped the Third World for its natural resources for their own gains. Despite arguments to the contrary, the American industrialization story is as callous and shameful as Europe's. The surplus of land the nation maintained was acquired through wars of aggression against a "mongrel race," Mexico, and various forms of blackmail, coercion, deceit, forced removal, or deadly force against Native communities. The nation's cheap labor came in the form of slavery in the South and in the North destitute immigrants from, first northern, then southern and eastern Europe fleeing the dehumanizing effects of industrialization in their homelands. In the West,

Mexicans and Asians, especially Chinese, became cogs in the American industrial machine, serving "faithfully" in mining camps under the most deplorable of conditions. Thus, Americans are also subject to the same colonizer discourse aimed at lessening the burden of guilt for two centuries of abusive behavior towards people of color. All the problems associated with a colonialist mentality will manifest themselves in American culture.

In his novel, *La Maravilla*, the Chicano writer Alfredo Véa, Jr. describes a conversation between a grandfather and his grandson that acts as an example the role the colonizer mentality plays in American society. The old man reminds the boy of the vacuous context of American culture,

"They...become other names and have no connection to places they live. They say they are one-third this and one-quarter that and their ancestors came from such and such, but they don't know nothing about them. They have no stories. They have no tribe. Their camp fire is the goddamn television."[16]

Véa has consolidated into one small passage America's most critical psychological concerns that both Franz Fanon and Albert Memmi consider critical to colonizer rule. The colonialist mentality submerged deep in the national subconscious manifests itself through various hollow sounding pretenses and masks meant to convince oneself of his/her privileged status as an American.

Because they must convince themselves that they are legitimate heirs to lands and resources of the United States, as Fanon and Memmi have argued, Americans must invent a past emphasizing white (colonizer) ascendancy over people of color. As this history is passed down from generation to generation the invented past becomes the factual present. Richard Drinnon and Richard Slotkin have described in great detail the development of an American national myth predicated on the violent domination of people of color. This manufactured truth has served the nation as a guide

25

by which its citizens view their relationship with the rest of the world, especially people of color.

Having no real connection to place, and without legitimate stories to secure their rights to the land, twentieth century Americans used the hypnotically powerful effects of cinema and television to tell and retell the stories of usurpation so that the national myth can live on in behalf of the nation's citizens. Just as Natives exercise the campfire as a place to remind the "People" of their connection to past, present and future, America has turned the theaters and television sets into compartmentalized campfires where the national myth is passed on to the next generation of naïve and unsuspecting Americans. It is these trusting souls that help in sustaining the most important feature in the colonialist mentality, what race historian Frank Tucker described nearly four decades ago as the White Conscience.

Although Tucker's work was first published in 1967, his christening of specific colonizer behavior as related to a racialized construct of the "other" eliminates the obscure relationship between colonialism and racism. The racist behavior of Americans occurring over the nation's history, propagandized to the American consumer in a less harsh more paternalistic voice in literature and cinema, is directly correlated to the colonizer-motivated language by which history has been recorded. The historical meta-narrative identified by Slotkin and Drinnon contributes to the interpretive tools by which white/colored relations are explained in this society. Throughout the nation's history events and movements saturated by white supremacist ideology are shrouded by colonizer language.[17] Retold generation after generation to children in schools as text or during a Saturday matinee as film, Americans become immune to negative effects the "outdated" white supremacist ideology carries in today's world.

The argument of race scholars such as Tucker, Thomas Gladwin and Ahmad Saidin,[18] writing in the

1960s and 1970s still hold true in today's world, albeit without the sophisticated language promulgated by post-modernist theorist in more recent years. In fact, at a time when Americans wholeheartedly support the unprovoked invasion of a nation of people of color and defend U.S. actions as a duty to bring Western-style democracy to an oppressed population, the White (sub)Conscience has never been put to better use than on this splendid occasion. Homogenizing two separate events, 9/11 and U.S. failed efforts to control a third-rate dictator, under the syllogistic argument that if 9/11 was perpetrated by Arab Muslims, and if Arab Muslims live in Iraq, therefore Iraq was at fault for the tragedy in New York and the United States is justified in invading the Arab nation. This kind of thinking comes from a society that continues to see race as the single-most important factor determining their welfare, yet the White (sub)Conscience allows them to deny any racial intolerance, because Americans have convinced themselves it does not exist. Invoking the principles identified by Drinnon and Slotkin, American aggressive behavior is identified as a response to an unprovoked attack by "Indians," or a pre-emptive strike against some imminent threat.

When country/western singers such as Toby Keith and Clint Black release such jingoist, and blatantly anti-Arab, songs as "Courtesy of the Red, White, and Blue" and "Iraq and Roll," and the country/western fiddle-playing icon Charlie Daniels questions the loyalty of Hollywood artists protesting the invasion of Iraq, it is obvious that this country continues to wallow, either in the ignorance of distinguishing between immediate threats, or, in the racist ideology that allows them to lump all people of color into one immediate, and continuous threat. The more likely scenario is that they suffer from both. The invasion of Iraq gave Americans the forum to express their deep-seated racist beliefs. Keith's abhorrent "Courtesy of the Red, White, and Blue" states, "Now this nation that I love has fallen

27

under attack. A mighty sucker punch came flying in from somewhere in the back. Soon as we could see clearly through our big black eye, Man we lit up your world like the Fourth of July."[19]

George W. Bush and his bellicose cohorts manufactured "weapons of mass destruction" and a connection between the perpetrators of 9/11 and Iraq to send American forces into Iraq. American leader's reluctance to distinguish between Arab communities and terrorist organizations is an example of the continued use of Slotkin's "Gunfighter Nation" trope. Released as a morale booster for the American troops invading Iraq, Keith's song sustains a mentality that justifies, and defends, unprovoked U.S. aggression against nations made up of people of color. Keith's failure to specifically identify Iraqis as the target of American punishment is a result of the old colonizer axiom Albert Memmi once vilified as "the mark of the plural."[20] "The mark of the plural" identifies individual human qualities (both good and bad) as generically held attributes of Natives as a whole; thus the actions of one individual are referred to in the plural pronoun "they."

Keith does not care if the Iraqi people were at fault for the attack of 9/11. Although his government leaders had convinced him that the 9/11-Iraqi link justified the nation's actions, actual proof of this connection was never confirmed. When "we lit up your world like the Fourth of July" Keith's only concern was that his nation had launched a military campaign against an enemy his leaders told him are a danger to his, and his countrymen's, safety. Because the threat came from a place inhabited by "them," Keith patriotically penned a work with such hateful language without questioning the validity of American government's evidence. The Iraqi people became Keith's twenty first century Indian. Not fully informed as to why he needed to know why his nation attacked Iraq, it sufficed that his leaders told him such was the case: the White (sub)Conscience defends the flimsiest of justifications as legitimate reason to attack "Indians."

The white leaders of the United States placed a blanket identity of "enemy" on those nations failing to support the American war against terrorism. When the white nations of Germany, France and Russia failed to back the U.S. invasion of Iraq, identified by the U.S. as a blow against terrorism, the U.S. exchanged accusations and insults, never bullets. The context by which Americans pick and choose friends and enemies is predicated on race, and yet we are able to deny this is the case. The White (sub)Conscience acts as the shield, defending the nation's right to act without any regard for the rights of people of color.

As earlier mentioned, Alfredo Vea's analogizes the campfire and the television. For many Native communities steeped in the oral tradition, the campfire is the place where stories are told, and the mores and values that hold the community together are told. During the twentieth century, first in theaters, and later at home, cinema and television acted as the American campfire. It was in these meetings that Americans received a civics lesson as the mesmerizing, and entertaining, storytelling played itself out on the screen. The subliminal power of cinema has molded the racial concepts of Americans so thoroughly they cannot even begin the filtering process to extricate themselves from the racist quagmire they live in.

In the fall of 2003, California was subjected to the political farce that was the Governor Gray Davis recall. During the campaign the populist candidate, the well-known and popular actor Arnold Schwarzenegger, to undermine his rival, targeted Indian gaming as one of the threats to the economic survival of the state.[21] Understanding that the candidate is a European immigrant, and not fully knowledgeable of U.S. history, one might excuse this antiquated and racist attack against Natives. However, the problem is that neither his rival, nor his supporters cared to address the racist connotation of the candidate's accusation. Needless to say, the candidate's message was a blatant pandering to the White (sub)Conscience of California voters.

In 2004 the governor vetoed a bill that would have banned the use of the name *Redskins* in five California high schools. Schwarzenegger claimed that local school districts should make their own choices. Opponents of the bill argued tradition warranted maintaining the name. One school official even went so far as to claim the decision allowed for the community and school "to keep something they hold in the highest esteem."[22] Neither the governor nor supporters of the name *Redskins* consider their position anti-Native American or racist.

Immune to racist ideology because it is represented as reality through film and television, Americans, in this case, Californians, accept racist, and white supremacist, rhetoric without questioning how the language harms Native people psychologically, and shapes mainstream perceptions of Natives and excuses damaging acts against them. As a key component in the influential and highly effective American pop culture, film continues to shape the minds and ideas of its audience today, and most probably will far into the future. How Americans see people of color, and in the case of this work, more specifically Native Americans, continues to be a manifestation of their ignorance of Native cultures. Faced with few desires to exert any energy to investigate these "foreign" cultures, Americans continue to rely on film as their window into the world of the "other."

Understanding the role cinema plays in the sustaining of the White (sub)Conscience is the first step in developing new principles and philosophies by which Hollywood can depict Native cultures, and assist in destroying the racist ideology that fuels U.S. policy, not only domestically, but abroad. As long as Americans continue to believe the misrepresentations of Native peoples Hollywood produced during the twentieth century, true Native American sovereignty will exist only in name, rather than in practice. As a child growing up with Hollywood's Indian representations, my image of Indians followed that of the mainstream.

Thus, as I choose the films to analyze the Hollywood/White Conscience relationship, the viewing list comes from my childhood memories. If it is true that I received a normal upbringing, and therefore, can be considered to have experienced an average childhood, the westerns I watched represent a cross-section of films America's baby-boomer generation was exposed to as children. Why should I search the archives of films I never viewed, to interpret them from the mind of a middle-aged educated male? I seek to understand why I valued these films as a child, and only now have begun to scrutinize the insensitive content in the work. Only my "childhood Indians" can remind me of the informal racist indoctrination I received as countless Indians hit the ground, killed by my white heroes. This study seeks to expose the endurance of the highly racialized White (sub)Conscience ideology sustained through a series of generations through Hollywood westerns' misrepresented use of Indian images.

The use of blatantly negative Indian images to argue this point is far too obvious, and academically unchallenging at this point in time. The Friars, Bataille and Silet, Churchill, Hilger, Singer and many others have already capably done this. Although failing to highlight the significant effect race has played in the development of negative Indian imagery in film, these many fine works have examined and criticized this practice. Rather than focus on the obvious, this study's focus is to explain the continued exposure of the White (sub)Conscience Indians in Hollywood's alleged "good Indian" characterizations during the half century after the end of World War II. I argue that these films, too, bolster American assumptions about race. The subliminal mind of America steadfastly holds on to the concepts of a threatening and inferior, albeit sometimes

31

noble and exotic, Indian. Therefore, this study will examine those films I grew up watching Saturday afternoons, or on the late show (only after my parents went to sleep) when I found the strength to keep awake. Some of the films were box office successes; others were B movie bombs. Nonetheless, they were the films I, and my contemporary generation, knew as our most reliable resource to the Indian-way. Whether it was John Wayne's Captain Kirby York, in *Ft. Apache* (1948), claiming that the Apaches were the greatest light cavalry on the face of the Earth, or Guy Madison's Miles Archer, in *The Charge at Feather River* (1953), explaining the reason Cheyennes refused to attack at night was because they were afraid if they were killed at night they couldn't find the Happy Hunting Grounds, we knew it was the truth. We knew it was the truth because Richard Drinnon's "Man Who Knows Indians,"[23] the authoritative white male who understood Indians better than even Indians did about themselves, told us.

To further argue the durability of the White (sub)Conscience, and its ability to survive under the harshest attacks from the civil rights movements of the 1950s and '60s and/or multi-cultural diversity of the 1970s, 80s and 90s, a cross-section of contemporary Indian imagery in films not related to "my childhood Indians" will be examined as well. These films include blockbuster epic tributes to Indian culture, such as *Dances With Wolves*, to less recognized, yet highly racially charged made for television films such as *Miracle in the Wilderness* (1992). A common denominator all these films share is the belief that they are paying homage to Native Americans and depicting them in realistic fashion.

Although the costumed Indian may be accurate, the Indian/white relationship continues to defend the White (sub)Conscience's racial, physical, and cultural superiority over Indians. What is most problematic about this behavior is that both the producer and consumer of the final product (the film) see no error in

32

their views. This mind-set is at the heart of the problem. The irony of this situation is that unbeknownst to the filmmakers and film audience, their behavior sustains the very ideas and beliefs of the extremist white supremacist organizations they are appalled by, and battle in the courts and legislatures to destroy. The subtle and low-keyed depiction of white supremacy in film provides the ideal pretense American society needs to defend its own form of the white myth.

American society can denounce the extremist hate mongers publicly and laud itself for legislation alleged producing equality or unified marches on Washington, but when the lights are dimmed and the entertainment begins, we still want to see the great white male saving the damsel, or humanity, from the savage creature. As one of the nation's most recognized "savage creatures" none better serves as the basis of this study than Native Americans, more specifically "Indians."[24]

This study is divided into five parts, each examining a critical component of the subtle effects Indian imagery in film has had on the subliminal mind of American society. In effect these images create a de facto segregated society where whiteness maintains its racist social value; beginning with chapter two, titled *The White (sub)Conscience*, introduces this divisive ideology as the White (sub)Conscience, a belief system predicated on an inconspicuous racist message resulting from the negative depiction of people of color in film. The White (sub)Conscience has its origins in the cultural misappropriation of Indian-ness by American culture. Beginning with the seventeenth century captivity-narratives of Mary Rowlandson, Indians were a critical component in American literature. During the nineteenth century literary forms from important plays, to dime novels reformulated and defined the standard Indian trope. By the time the American film industry became a profitable capitalist entity, the Indian image had been fully developed and necessitated only subtle modifications to maintain its social significance.

In chapter three, *Holding the Fort* I examine Indian imagery in 1930s and '40s Hollywood that act as the vanguard for my "Childhood Indian" experience. These are the westerns that will dominate late night and Saturday afternoon programming and entertain not only its cinema screen audience, but also a generation of innocuous baby-boomers. Westerns produced during the 1930s and '40s transferred the Indian from its literary and silent film era form to the silver screen while maintaining much of the representation's metaphoric significance. While turning the Indian into a legitimate box office strategy, Hollywood was able to hold true to the literary Indian image. Mass audiences of Americans were now able to see and hear the blood curdling Indian they had only read about in dime novels, or as part of one of the many Wild West shows popular at the turn of the century. Now it was possible for viewers to actually see the frontier saga unfold before their very eyes in the comfort of a theater. Most importantly, what Americans believed as part of the frontier mythology, to be their Indian, continued to exist in celluloid form. The Indian had made the transition from book to silver screen without losing its social significance and thus allowing future generations of film makers the opportunity to continue misappropriating the image to serve their commercial interests.

The fourth chapter, *The "Good" Indian Film: Dependent Natives and Great Fathers*, analyzes the "new" and "innovative" Indian of post-World War II Hollywood. While innovative in the sense that the "new" Indian is depicted in a more favorable light, the images still preserve the culturally acceptable dependency of Natives on the technologically and morally superior White male figures. Influenced by generations of literary and cinematic concepts of Natives, Hollywood creates Indian images that are firmly entrenched in the national subconscious. Thus,

34

critically acclaimed films such as *Broken Arrow* (1950), and other 1950s "good" Indian films, develop only a superficially "New" Indian. Racialized perceptions of Natives persisted in films lauded for breakthrough cinematic characterizations. The White (sub)Conscience's influence was too strong to permit the film industry to depict "innovatively" independent, complex and morally principled Natives without contrasting these with the more recognizable savage and deceitful Indian.

Proving more complex and problematic than the paternalistic and colonizer mentality Indian image is what I refer to as the "context" Indian film. These films maintain elements of both concepts of Indian while addressing contemporary political or social issues. In chapter five, *Serving the Nation Proudly: the Allegoric Indian, Cold War, Civil Rights and Vietnam*, political and social ideology was woven into the narrative of westerns. Indians served as the symbolic counterpoint to the issue inspiring the films production. The Indian was a hindrance in the context of these films. They served as a background prop permitting the storyline to highlight the Cold War, Civil Rights and Vietnam arguments. Regardless, Cold War, Civil Rights and Vietnam allegory, the cinematic Indian upheld the finest tradition of the White (sub)Conscience.

By the end of the Civil Rights Movement the allegoric Indian had served its purpose, yet Hollywood still continues to find a market for Indian films. Chapter six, *Lord John Morgan and Lt. John Dunbar to the Rescue: Revisionist Hollywood and Sustaining the White (sub)Conscience*, examines the continued use of the misrepresented Indian image at a time when state and corporate pressures for Native resources place a strain on Native sovereignty. Perhaps not in the same version that dominated the pre-World War II cinema, or survived the "context" use of the Cold War and Civil Rights era, but in this era of "multi-culturalism" and racial "diversity," America is only happy to continue viewing the Indian on screen, albeit still very much the "childhood" Indian variety. Fixated on the archaic images of Indians that literature and film have inculcated into the national conscience, Hollywood regurgitates anachronistic representations of Indians within contemporary concepts of alleged social egalitarianism. Films such as Kevin Costner's *Dances With Wolves* (1990) or Ron Howard's White-captivity saga *The Missing* (2003) uphold the consensus beliefs Americans have of the Indian. The "Childhood Indians" of these directors led them to sustain racialized and insulting images, even as they seek to depict Natives more honestly and realistically.

Costner, Howard and the dozens of other contemporary filmmakers who claim to depict Indians more realistically are hampered by the White (sub)Conscience's subliminal influence of racial constructs developed during their "Childhood Indian" experience. History suggests modern images of Natives extend the national concept of "Indian" to serve as a literary or cinematic buttress to preserve the nation's exploitative legacy. Even as the society revels in its rhetoric of "multi-culturalism" and racial diversity, the nations "Childhood Indian" generation sustains attitudes and beliefs that obfuscate racist sentiments about Native peoples.

Regardless of the suggested imagery, these feature presentations continue to spew the same racialized propaganda that earlier generations of American novelist and screenwriters have disseminated to the masses. Is it possible today for a nine-year old indigenous boy to play Cowboys and Indians in his backyard and root for the latter? Has society evolved sufficiently enough to remove the Indian stigma from the child? The problems America faces today are directly linked to the nation's failure to identify its paternalistic and bullying behavior towards people of color. An historical legacy of racialized indoctrination has proven itself too strong to be destroyed. Has the American institution of racism become so much a part of the national fabric that Americans are unable to accept that it has become an anachronism? The White (sub)Conscience suggests it has not.

[1] Cultural Studies scholar, Tom Englehardt had a similar experience as a child growing up in the 1950s. On page eighty-five of his study *The End of Victory Culture: Cold War America and the Disillusioning of a Generation* (1995) he describes a typical game of toy soldier war. "The crucial question was when to stop the killing of the bluecoats and begin the slaughter of the Indians," Englehardt adds, " Sometimes it was powerful enough that I found myself almost siding with the Indians. Yet it was a temptation I never brought myself to test out." Even though the thought of Indian victory crossed our minds, U.S. popular cultural upbringing prevented many of us from realizing the possibility of Indian victory.

[2] Ralph E. Friar and Natasha A. Friar, *The Only Good Indian...The Hollywood Gospel*, New York: Drama Book Specialists, (1972), 3.

[3] Friar, 6.

[4] Vine Deloria, *The Pretend Indians: Images of the Native Americans in the Movies*, edited by Gretchen Bataille and Charles Silet, Ames: The Iowa State University Press, (1980), xvi.

[5] The book is divided into five analytical sections and an annotated bibliography segment. The theoretical sections consist of "The Native American: Myth and Media Stereotyping," "The Indian in the Film: Early Views," "The Indian in the Film: Later Views," "Photographic Essay on the American Indian as Portrayed by Hollywood," and "Contemporary Reviews."

[6] Rita Keshena, "The Role of American Indians in Motion Pictures," *The Pretend Indians*, 109-110.

[7] Richard Schickel, "Why Indians Can't Be Villains Any More," *The Pretend Indians, 150.*

[8] The screenplay for *Ulzana's Raid* is suggested from the November/December 1885 real-life reservation-break of twelve disgruntled Chihenne and Chokonen (Chiricahua Apaches) warriors, led by Olzonne (sometimes referred in history books as Josanie); the younger brother of the Chihenne clan leader, Chihuahua. In the film, the death of Ulzana's son convinces the Indian his bloody adventure, like the fate of his people, is doomed to failure and in the end allows the (Good) Indian scout to execute him. In real life Olzonne will led the American Army on a two-month chase over twelve hundred miles, killing thirty-eight people, and wearing out over two hundred horses and mules, at a loss of only one member of his party. Olzonne returned to the San Carlos Reservation without any criminal repercussions. He survived long enough to be one of the over three-hundred Chiricahua Apaches to be forcibly removed from Arizona and New Mexico to Florida in 1886, beginning a twenty-seven year prisoner of war odyssey that ended in 1912.

[9] Schickel, 151.

[10] Michael Hilger, *From Savage to Nobleman: Images of Native Americans in Film*, Lanham, Maryland: The Scarecrow Press, (1995), 11.

[11] Ward Churchill, *Fantasies of the Master Race: Literature, Cinema and the Colonization of American Indians*, San Francisco: City Lights Books, (1998), x.

[12] Churchill, 134.

[13] As recent newspaper accounts indicates, Churchill is obsessed by Nazis, and seems to find them everywhere.

[14] Churchill, 142.

[15] Chinweizu, *The West and the Rest of Us: White Predators Black Slavers and the African Elite*, New York: Vintage Books, (1975), 14.

[16] Alfredo Vea, Jr., *La Maravilla*, New York: Plume, (1993), 35.

[17] A flaw in recording American history is the colonizer mentality use of euphemisms to describe distasteful events in the nation's past; e.g. free-labor system becomes a battle over workers' rights rather than the first de facto union to discriminate against people of color, Indians are "removed" rather than bullied off their land, and nineteenth century Indian Schools civilized students rather than performing cultural genocide.

[18] Gladwin and Saidin examine the various parts of colonialism in their 1980 collaborative work *Slaves of the White Myth*, spending considerable energy describing connection between the destructive nature of colonialism and the role the myth of white supremacy figures in maintaining social order.

[19] "Courtesy of the Red, White and Blue (The Angry American)," lyrics by Toby Keith, (2003).

[20] Albert Memmi, *The Colonizer and the Colonized*, London: Earthscan Publications, 1990 (c 1957), 151.

[21] Incidentally, as I began work on this chapter, rival agencies to Indian gaming began a smear campaign claiming that tribes were taking in revenues in excess of $8 billion yearly. The ads conveniently fail to include

the expenses Indian casinos incur and pay out from the $8 million revenues. Once again the subliminal racist dialogue identifies Indians as a threat to the existence of civilized people, in this case California taxpayers.

[22] Schwarzenegger: Yes to 'Redskins,' by Francie Grace, Associated Press, 9/22/2004.

[23] Drinnon writes of an American character that exists on the nation's frontier. These male figures travel into the unknown territories confronting the dangerous challenges of nature and helping to pave the way for civilization, more specifically American civilization. In their crusade to bring progress to the wilderness these men must take on the lifestyles and customs of the Indian inhabitants, and because of their innate intellectual superiority the white men actually out-Indian the Indians. Historical examples of these figures begin with Daniel Boone and are followed by men like Kit Carson, and most recently Edward Lansdale in Vietnam. All these figures assisted in opening "frontiers" for the United States, but it has been the literary, both literature and film, "man who knows Indians" that has carried on the legacy of these pioneering adventurers, and the imperialistic national agenda of Americans.

[24] As will be discussed later, the idea of Indian is a European invention; at no point in the pre-contact period did the inhabitants of the western hemisphere refer to themselves as Indians. Therefore I use the term Indian to identify the European, or more specifically American, image of Natives.

Chapter 2
The White (sub)Conscience:
If it's Invisible,
Then Racism No Longer Exist.

Race theorist David Theo Goldberg introduces the first chapter of his critically acclaimed work, *Racist Culture* (1993), with the epigraph, "Individuals may well come and go; it seems that philosophy travels nowhere."[1] Goldberg uses this quote to explain the continued existence of a racist dogma associated with a bygone era in contemporary America. Regardless of social movements that typical Americans believe have eliminated the need to debate, or even suggest, the existence of racism today, archaic ideas continue to affect a new generation of citizens; that in the long run condemns society to live by the philosophies adhered to in an earlier era. Living today in a world of "political-correctness" and "multi-culturalism," the idea that race theory can still scrutinize American society appears anachronistic. Goldberg argues,

> The prevailing view concerning contemporary racism is that it is something that belongs to the past. Where it is taken to occur at all, it is considered as socially anomalous, as unusual, an individual aberration.... Anyone extending to racist expression a greater place in contemporary culture than this picture warrants is bound to be considered paranoid.[2]

Within Goldberg's interpretation of mainstream American race theory, this study is out of context with contemporary scholarship. Yet, I find myself inexplicitly drawn to this notion that somehow American society has deluded itself into believing its version of multiculturalism and diversity benefits all members of society, and those that fail to advance beyond their current economic or social standing have only themselves to blame. The answer to this question is concealed within the long history of a people who have adapted racist discourse to resolve contemporary political or social debates, unrepentant of its treatment of Native Americans.

Americans have created a visual picture of the nation that is founded on over two hundred years of racialized language depicting Native inferiority. During the second half of the twentieth century, pressured by Third World wars of liberation and its own civil rights movement, the United States has sought to distance itself from this previous ideology. Despite the nation's history of oppression and violence perpetrated against people of color from which there exist a plethora of incidents, in recent decades Americans have insulated themselves from reality by creating a fantasy society devoid of racial biases. Within this societal logic, the social inequalities that are drawn along color lines can be easily argued away by the descendants of a people who have at various points in their history, maintained Blacks as slaves, bullied their neighbor to the south into a war that resulted in the acquisition of half of Mexico's land, sustained the forced removal of Native Americans, or at times the more expedient policy of genocide. As twenty-first century America addresses the nation's racial concerns, a majority White society, and its mutually inclusive culture, determine the parameters by which race is discussed.

Thus, my dilemma, as this work seeks to explore the racialized imagery of Native Americans in cinema and television contributing to a racist social conscience; I find myself walking the fine line between academic scholarship and archaic paranoid discourse. The pundit will argue that race is no longer an issue and that society must move beyond the hurtful language of race that conjures up the old ghosts of the past. This argument does nothing more than sustain the very beliefs this work dares to confront. As our society advances forward on issues of technology, and increasing the standards of living for those capable of affording these new concepts, we continue to hold on to an ideology permitting society to enjoy their rewards without the guilt associated with exploiting other people.

Modern Euro-American society places value on the notion that individuals attain their highest level of success based on their personal efforts. These efforts are made possible by the liberal idealized principles of liberty, equality and fraternity. As western society places more and more emphasis on the effect of these factors within the community, "it increasingly insists upon the moral irrelevance of race."[4] Yet, the social discourse of the society claiming no use for race has over four hundred years of racialized behavior that have created the standards by which racial issues are addressed. The discourse of Frantz Fanon and his contemporaries anticipating post-colonialism have argued that the colonizer insists on denying responsibility for the depressed social conditions of people of color.

At the point of the publication of his timeless study, *The Wretched of the Earth* (1963), Fanon identified a period when three-quarters of the earth's population possessed the world, yet the other quarter of the population, "had the use of it."[5] The three-quarter to one-quarter ratio was based on race, with the former consisting of people of color, while the latter of Whites. The relationship between the two was (and still is) firmly rooted in the racially influenced oppression of dark-skinned people for the benefit of the White master race. As anti-colonialists such as Fanon argue, the denial of this relationship is fundamental to maintaining this system. Although race is the key factor affecting this relationship, claiming it is not makes the argument it *is*, irrelevant. Redefining Benjamin Disraeli's statement defending England's Anglo-Saxon racial superiority,[6] Goldberg astutely identifies the paradoxical context by which Americans see the race question, "Race is irrelevant, but all is race."[7]

Although by the 21st century Americans claim to have reached a social multi-culturalism that has reduced race to a non-factor, their means of entertainment will argue otherwise. Beginning with the captivity narratives of colonial America through the nineteenth century literary prose and twentieth century use of cinema, writers have consciously, or sub-consciously, expressed their own *Weltanschauung* within their work, or perhaps even their "civic virtue."[8] The world these people see is fraught with dangers inspired by the exotic cultures of Brown-skinned people threatening the very existence of civilization. It is from this social framework that writers expressed the social construct of the world by which he/she narrates their story. Raised in a society where imperialist behavior sustained by racist ideology masked by a colonizer language denying the existence of any wrongdoing, in turn generates a literary style that itself employed (and continues to employ) the very principles of colonialism Fanon and Memmi argue colonizers deny exist.

In his thoroughly researched and highly respected American Studies trilogy examining American literature and film, historian Richard Slotkin touches on a number of the reconstructed literary and cinematic forms Native Americans have appeared in over the course of the nation's history. As new methods of entertainment were employed to distract the masses, a dual subliminal social allegory provided the reader or viewer with vital information to function effectively in the ever-changing society. The larger context of Slotkin's trilogy explores the language contributing to a national "myth" based on an ever-present frontier. Even as Slotkin's work extends the scholarship of American Studies to new heights, his examination of the "myth" in American pop culture fails to explain the significance of this theme on the national conceptualization of people of color, especially Native Americans.

Those images of the Natives have appeared, and reappeared, in American literature and pop culture through various reincarnations. The duality of this image obfuscates and aids in the denial of wrongdoing, for as the lecherous, cruel, and indolent Indian wove itself through the national discourse, the noble, brave, and independent Indian sustained the image of a child-like existence and also merged itself deep into the national myth.[9] Each image provides the discussants with the vision of the Indian they deem sufficient to argue their point. Robert Berkhofer, Jr. describes this effect as *The White Man's Indian* where, "White interest in the American Indian surges and ebbs with the tides of history."[10] Indians have become the copyrighted property of mainstream America's national discourse, depending on the existing socio-political debate.

The late Choctaw-Cherokee scholar Louis Owens posits the notion that "Indians" are in fact a European creation and exist only in a Euro-American context. So pervasive is the myth of the "Indian" that even as Native Americans seek their own identity, the characteristics they use as a reference come from the Euro-American construct of "Indian-ness."[11] Thus the Native American paradox, realizing that Americans will only recognize the "real Indian" of Anglo-American iconography, Natives adopt these fictitious images in order to be accepted as "legitimate" representatives of their tribes.

Thus the concept of the "Indian" is truly an American invention. With this in mind, however, it is simpler to understand the origins of the Indian image in American culture, and why its metaphoric use has been dictated by mainstream beliefs. As a by-product of colonialism, the United States must confront its contemporary activities, especially towards people of color, with some recognition of its sinister past; thus, the social discourse of the nation is replete with the lexicon of denial. Every use of language by scholars, intellectuals, politicians, or religious figures containing Indian imagery has a fundamental defense of Americans aggressive and brutal behavior towards Natives built within the narrative: whether intended or not.

Although this work's concern is with exploring the use of alleged authentic Indian images in film to defend a repugnant ideology of racial and cultural supremacy, one cannot begin to appreciate the power of cinema without understanding the origins of Indian imagery as part of the national identity. The seeds of this practice were introduced early in American history and continue to affect national thought to this day.

The cataclysmic arrival of Columbus in the Americas truly signaled the beginning of a "new world," but newness based on racial ideology,[12] rather than the ridiculous concept of any "virgin land." Columbus' "discovery" set the foundation for modern-day colonialism, and the racialized language associated with American society's defense of the economic system helped create this nation's greatness at the expense of people of color. It is from these humble origins that the racist discourse of the American people is founded. Over the course of the next five hundred years American society would develop and refine the racialized beliefs by which the community could (and still can) justify its callous treatment of people of color; in the case of the United States, especially, Native Americans. The rationalizing will best be served by using the very images of those the nation seeks to abuse. The language of power will utilize the representations of Native Americans, the Indian, or the national (mis)representation of what Americans believe the Native American to be at any given moment in the history of the United States.

During the colonial era Indians gave writers such as Increase Mather, the ultimate antagonist to contrast their narrative of the "Saints" struggle as God's "chosen people."[13] In his critique of American society's misuse of Indian imagery, historian Robert Berkhofer, Jr., uses the concept of "Puritan, the Wilderness, and Savagery as Divine Metaphors" to explain the Puritan perception of their New World existence.[14] Mary Rowlandson's narrative, first published in 1682, aptly titled, *The Sovereignty and Goodness of God, Together with the Faithfulness of His Promise Displayed* suggests her capture by, and subsequent escape from, Indians was God's test of a woman who had developed a complacency for the strict virtues of Puritan life.[15] Rowlandson's experience with the savages cleansed her of her sins. It also reminded the Puritan reader of the constant threat the wilderness posed to the Saints in their quest to establish their "citty upon the hill" in the New World.

To the colonial era Puritan writers, Indians functioned as the beast-like entities by which God judged the Saints. According to Slotkin, "In the captivity narratives, bestial Indians are seen as the outward type of the beast that is in every man." He continues, "The captive, too, hunts a beast in the forest...the captive's salvation depends on his ability to see that the 'hellish principles' are within himself."[16] As the New England colonists recorded the histories of the two most cataclysmic encounters between the Natives and Europeans of the region, the Pequot War (1637-1638) and King Phillip's Wars (1676-1677), the events served as history lesson and symbol of spiritual piety. In both interpretations it is vital to the Saints that they eliminate the Indians, whether as the perceived mortal threat, or the demon within.

Richard Drinnon, a historian praised for his innovative study linking American expansionism and racism, argues in *Facing West* (1990), that the literary significance of Indians goes beyond the simple social parable. The native in fact, validates America's existence. "...[W]ithout Indians," he argues, "the forefathers would have had no way to prove themselves in trials by ordeal as they wrested the wilderness from the stiffening red hands."[17] Without the Indian, God has no way of testing virtuous Christians. Lakota scholar, Vine Deloria, Jr., maintains, "Christian religion and the Western idea of history are inseparable and mutually self-supporting."[18] Like the community it seeks to empower, the literary appropriation of Indian imagery to defend Eurocentric aggression against the Natives will thrive and progress through time of civilization according to the social needs.

When not employed as symbols to justify colonialist exploitation of Natives, the Indian image became the property of Americans debating political issues. The Indian dressed Bostonians dumping of English tea in Boston Harbor in 1774 is a national icon suggesting American political discontent and the onset of the revolutionary fervor that culminated in the birth of the United States. The Delaware sachem Tamenend, the man who gave William Penn the opportunity to buy Native lands, became Saint Tammany and fostered the creation of the Sons of St. Tammany societies. These uses of Indian imagery introduce the American tradition of (mis)appropriating Indian images for social or political needs. In neither case are the Indian figures representing American principles meant to incorporate real Indians into the political, or social, movement the White organizers are seeking to recognize. The Indian provides the iconography to develop a concept exclusively for White Americans. The images that were developed helped to establish an American identity that political leaders could define as fresh and without the stains of corruption from European culture.

The Indian of the Revolutionary War era sustained new concepts of an American identity. As Philip Deloria explains, "Increasingly inclined to see themselves in opposition to England rather than Indians, they [the American colonists] inverted interior and exterior…. They began to transform exterior, noble savage Others into symbolic figures that could be rhetorically interior to the society they sought to inaugurate."[19] The Indian was the conduit by which rebellious colonists transformed themselves from European settlers to American republicans. Even as actual Native American peoples faced the ever-expanding American desire for land, the "Indian" became an integral part of the American social discourse.[20] During the remainder of the eighteenth-century, while frontier America supported a policy of extermination of Native Americans, for Eastern intellectuals and political leaders the Indian embodied the best virtues of republicanism,[24] and as the nation began its westward march beginning with Thomas Jefferson's Louisiana Purchase in 1803, the Indian experienced an enigmatic, and ever-changing, identity during the next century.

Descendants of the age of enlightenment, Jeffersonian Americans had accepted Indians as nature's children at their most fundamental existence. Contemporary scholars described the Indians with language depicting them as 'free and independent,' and living on instinct. Their government was based not on codes, but on 'habits and customs;' they "lacked the insecurity and self-doubt that civilization had saddled upon the white man."[21] Yet, it was the Native's very connection with nature that contributed to early nineteenth-century American ambivalent imagery of Indians. Many of the republican virtues attached to Natives were still present amongst eastern Indian reformers, but the question of whether Natives could adapt to American society became even more of an issue as U.S. aspirations for expansion became more prominent. It was during the Jeffersonian era that the "Vanishing American" Indian gained in popularity. Early nineteenth-century philanthropists held on to the notion that nature's child could somehow be incorporated into U.S. society, but even Jefferson was making plans for the eventual removal of Natives from their ancestral homes.

The first "great American benefactor" to the Indians, Jefferson wrote a series of letters in 1792 to the British minister, George Hammond, debating international claims. Jefferson made references to respecting the rights to soil only in the case of white nations, but not to Indians. Hammond posited that Jefferson planned to "exterminate the Indians and take the lands."[22] Despite reassurances from Jefferson that his responsibilities to the Indians was actually to protect them, "Less than two decades later, before Jefferson handed over the presidency to Madison, white America had acquired through purchase and otherwise 109,884,000 acres of Indian land."[23] As Jefferson, "the protector of Indian rights," defended his charges, he also found time to remove them from their native lands, placing many of the Chickasaws (1805) and the Choctaws and some Cherokees (1808) in far-off lands where the Indians were expected to become good citizens.[24] The lust for land proved too tempting even for the most ardent Indian supporter. It proved easier to develop literary Indian images depicting them as the last of a dying breed.

By the 1830s, within the context of Manifest Destiny Indians still provided the backdrop to lecture social values to mid nineteenth-century American readers. While these iconographies received mass support in the east, and continued to extol the virtuous Anglo-Saxon battle against the wilderness, subtle changes were in the making. By 1826 only one of the Declaration of Independence signatories still lived. Historian George Forgie argues that the mere presence of the founding fathers helped sustain the nation's new identity. Susan Scheckel adds that as the figures disappeared and "individuals actually responsible for

52

creating the nation faded into the past," intellectuals of the post-Revolutionary period sought new means to define the national identity.[25] As these Revolutionary figures died it became more difficult to employ living iconography to recognize a national ancestry. The mere existence of figures that reminded people of their revolutionary origins became obsolete; the need for more creative reminders of social responsibilities made literature an even more important source of national dialogue than it had before the nation gained its independence.

To writers of the 1830 and 1840s Natives helped define a nineteenth-century role for the United States. Reginald Horsman astutely incorporates the social construct of the Indian image into the doctrine of Manifest Destiny. Long identified as obstacles to progress, the Indian now became the foil to western expansion. Even their alter-ego "noble savage" identity could no longer save them from the march of civilization. Writing at the end of the eighteenth century, Hugh Henry Brackenridge, the first significant American writer from the trans-Appalachian West, published works describing the Natives in much more virulent terms than many of his contemporaries. His were the Indians of the "real" West; they did not possess any of the "noble" qualities eastern writers and philanthropists saw in the Natives. Brackenridge's Indians held the frontiersman's image of their "savage" rival. These were the animal-like creatures devoid of human qualities. Brackenridge identified Indian characteristics that best supported expansionist concepts.[26] "In the states that confronted the Indian…the Indian was often regarded as an expendable inferior savage," Horsman continues, "They did not want a government civilization policy that perpetuated Indians on their lands. They wanted to expel Indians, not transform them."[27]

During the Jacksonian Period, 1828-1850, America was in the nascent phase of its nineteenth-century westward expansion, and its literature required language supporting the forcible removal of Natives from their traditional homelands and circumventing national accountability for these acts. Literature maintained strong racialized imagery that was capable of defending the nation's ambivalence towards Native's human rights. During this era, whether the hero was John Filson's fictitious Daniel Boone, James Fenimore Cooper's Natty Bumppo, or Ned Buntline's literary Buffalo Bill Cody, the reader was reminded of the cultural, physical and racial superiority of the protagonist over the Native. In Filson's 1790s Daniel Boone narratives, his works center on an agrarian utopia where an age of enlightenment allegory explores the development of the consummate republican citizen in the wilderness.[28] While Daniel Boone is the embodiment of this virtuous figure, the Indian represents the victory of the wilderness over "man's better nature."[29] In this literary depiction the Natives are too weak to defeat and conquer the wilderness, only the more advanced American culture can defeat the wilderness and earn the right to use this land. Indians provide the contrast for the reader to fully understand the immensity of the American accomplishment.

James Fenimore Cooper's Leatherstocking series (1823-41) creates a complex figure in Natty Bumppo that assisted in developing the national myth that Richard Slotkin has so meticulously examined. The series narratives allow for literary debates on social, political, religious, and racial levels from an American perspective. Using the mythological American frontiersman as the centerpiece of his work, Cooper was helping to establish the national identity Americans had been so desperately seeking since the end of the American Revolution; an image that challenged the European character and sliced away any umbilical connection to the Old World.[30] Critical to this identity was the Native American. Like his contemporaries Cooper employed his Indians as an image to juxtapose their dying (vanishing), monolithic culture versus the vibrant, complex, albeit flawed, American society.

In *The Pioneers* (1823) Cooper suggests the nation can come to terms with its future by rebuilding over the past with new heirs to power. This goal proves problematic as the very foundation upon which contemporary America exists is built on the past; thus, as Natty Bumppo refuses to join the new generation of Americans, he, like the nation "drifts away toward the setting sun, running from but never escaping its past."[31] According to Cooper, regardless of how far America ventures into the unknown wilderness, it can never escape its past. The more removed from their European origins the better off Americans would be. Writers such as Cooper appropriated the symbolic Indian heritage to help foster a western hemispheric origin for the United States. To these writers, the nation's westward expansion is nothing less than the reclaiming of a family heirloom.

Bumppo's escape into the wilderness to get away from civilization is the futile attempt of an old man to hide from his, in a literary and national sense, obligation to bring progress to the continent. Little solace was Bumppo's fate to the castrated Indian Chingachcook, who in his death symbolized the emasculation of a people who were in the process of losing their land to American expansion. Like the European legends that tied the productivity of the land to its king, the castrated Indian no longer had the virility to use the lands.[32] It was the Manifest Destiny of the young and dynamic United States to take the lands from the decrepit and unproductive Natives to bring life (civilization) to the region.

During the middle-half of the nineteenth-century Native Americans were subjected to an all out assault on their mortal existence. By whatever means necessary, political manipulation, coercion, or military force, most Native Americans living east of the Mississippi River lost their indigenous lands to White Americans by the start of the Civil War. Literature and theater of the era suggested the actions of Americans were morally justified. Scheckel argues that in addition to Cooper's *The Pioneers*; George Custis's immensely popular play, *Pocahontas, or The Settlers of Virginia, A National Drama* (1836), helped to ameliorate any guilty feelings over removal of Natives from their traditional homelands.

The nineteenth-century stage Pocahontas helped define the national identity; the character of Pocahontas worked a dual metaphor justifying rights of conquest and to establish an American birthright to the land. As the indigenous virgin female who gives herself freely to the conquering European (Rolfe), she clarified the age-old issue affecting the colonizer's right to usurp and rule the lands of Native peoples. By choosing a European over the many (inferior) warriors vying for her hand in marriage, Pocahontas, the metaphoric virgin land, gave herself voluntarily to the submission, and rule, of the English. Because of her "royal" heritage, Pocahontas's actions legitimized American rights to the land; including those in contestation at present (Cherokee and Indian Removal).

In addition to her land rights symbol, Pocahontas also provided the mother figure, and subsequent national identity, post-Revolutionary America had long struggled to attain. As the wife of Rolfe, the English colonist, Pocahontas embodies "the sanctified figure of the nation-as-mother who unites all her citizens/children in a unified 'family.'"[33] By the time Indian Removal began in earnest in the late-1830s, and the nation battled to come to terms with an Indian policy that failed to protect the negotiated treaty rights of Natives, and it embarked on a holy mission to extend its borders and culture into the sovereign territory of its "Red Brothers," *Pocahontas* assuaged any guilt. The patriotic melodrama served to reinforce the colonizer concepts of Native inferiority, while helping to forge a national identity.

The colonizer mentality is a critical component of American expansionism; without a concept of racial and cultural faults attributable to the Natives, Americans had no justifiable reason to challenge Native ownership of the land. One of Edgar Allan Poe's less acclaimed works, a periodical serial appearing in *Burton's Gentlemen's Magazine* in 1840 titled, "The Journal of Julius Rodman" has been described by John Carlos Rowe as *"imperial fantasy."*[34] Although the work describes the fictionalized journal account of one man's adventure into the American frontier, it is also very much an endorsement of U.S. expansion into the newly acquired Louisiana Territory. At a time when the nation was developing a "manifest destiny" identity demanding the forced removal of Indians from their traditional homelands and the seizure of its Mexican neighbor's border region the *imperial fantasy* narrative contributed a valuable affirmation of these ideas. While critics will never place this work in the same category as Poe's classic works, "The Journal of Julius Rodman" does contain a strong dose of anti-Indian racial imagery that supports the developing national racial conscience. It can be described as typical of the social discourse developed in the literature of the period and it bolsters Manifest Destiny ideas. Poe's work has his hero, Julius Rodman, making a Lewis and Clarkesque expedition into Oregon territory in 1791-1794, relying on the previously published works of Washington Irving, Nicholas Biddle, John K. Townsend, and Meriwether Lewis's diary for most of his historical information.[35]

Regardless of from whom Poe received his background material, the manner in which events are recorded in the "Journal" is most definitively Poe's. His description of characters of color reflects the Southern gentlemanly quality he identified himself with; the region of the nation most associated with Manifest Destiny and the uniform removal of all Indians from their traditional homelands to west of the Mississippi River. Poe assumed the nation's westward expansion was most assuredly justified by race. Southern scholars and politicians had been spewing out a steady stream of works defending slavery by the time "Journal" was published, and a significant element of their arguments extended itself to the "idea of the innate inequality of the races."[36] Rodman's slave, Toby, was described in the archetypal stereotyped language of Southern society, emphasizing the slave's "swollen lips, large white protruding eyes, flat nose, long ears, double head, pot-belly, and bow legs."[37] Poe's fantasy description of the Natives followed the similar racialized bias.

According to Poe the "physical ugliness of the Sioux is matched only by their stupidity."[38] When Rodman turns a deck cannon on the Natives, the American is able to convince the naïve Lakota that the weapon is a tool of the "Great Spirit" and in his anger at the Natives the God desires the White man to fire at a crowd of on-looking villagers. Twenty-four Natives are killed or wounded by the cannon; an incident Rodman's conscience will easily deal with. Poe also emphasized the aggressive nature of the Indians, and suggested that their inherently violent behavior contributed to a decline in their numbers. Thus, the Vanishing American myth was linked to the Indians' own destructive conduct. Rowe refers to this as "historical revisionism" that "displaces the violence of Euro-American colonization onto the 'inherent' tribal violence of 'primitive' native peoples."[39] In the social ideology of Manifest Destiny, Poe's Indians displayed the subhuman traits that justified their sacrifice, and eventual demise, for the sake of American expansion and Progress.

By the 1830s, the language of the frontier symbolism—wilderness, savages, and virgin land—was merged and substituted by a more industrial metaphor. As early as the mid-nineteenth century intellectuals had begun modernizing the age-old vision, with the message now emphasizing a secular context for expansion and conquest. In the 1830s, the Whig orator, Edward Everett, described the west as "a safety valve to the great social steam engine."[40] Using the vernacular of Charles Darwin, American expansionist doctrine was "evolving" into a more advanced stage. The principles of democracy had become synonymous with "the American nation" and the Anglo-Saxon race.

The Indian wars of the 1870s further advanced the principle, as Colonel George Armstrong Custer's Dakota Territory experience shows in particular. The ruthless war the U.S. military waged against the Lakota doubled, not only as a war of imperialism necessary for the extending of American democratic principles, but also as a metaphor of the nation's emerging class struggle. The mass media employed Custer as a symbol imbued with the virtues of America's "best classes," responsible for revitalizing the nation's prosperity.[41]

Custer's ignominious defeat at the hands of the northern Plains tribes' alliance became a national metaphor for the impending social class struggle brought on by the increasing number of "undesirable" immigrants from eastern and southern Europe coming to the United States. Works such as future secretary of state, John Hay's *The Breadwinner* (1885) employed language depicting the working-class immigrants similarly to that used to describe Native Americans only a few decades earlier. Like the Indians of a previous literary age, an American puts the immigrant worker-class in its place. In this case, former Civil War officer Arthur Farnham gains his experience in the West, but his high-society upbringing prevents his being consumed by the frontier, as it had many previous White adventurers whom had helped forge the way for civilized settlers.[42] The savage and uncivilized manners of the immigrants condemned them to second-class status. The newly arrived immigrants from southern and eastern Europe, devoid of many of the characteristics and customs nativist Americans could relate to, like the Indian, became the new social metaphor that contrasted the evils of ignorance against the moral superiority of industrial capitalism. That Americans had little use for immigrants, other than as cogs in the national industrial machine, was one feature of the accepted ideology fueling the country's social conscience. Within a couple of generations immigrants would purchase "whiteness" and assimilate (to a degree), taking their place in the White society that still excluded Natives.

In a brief essay published in 1978 Richard Drinnon introduces an idea pre-dating the 1980 "Indian-hating" theory he so brilliantly argues in *Facing West*. Drinnon appropriates the Anglo-Saxon imperialist canon "White Man's Burden" into "Red Man's Burden," thus creating a more appropriate social concept of the "Indian" at *fin-de-cicle*.[43] The Indian-hating concept he argues allowed Americans to employ the threat of Indians as a justification for imperialist wars of expansion against Native Americans, and that when the nation's economic and social woes of the 1890s forced it to seek new territories to fix its problems, the language could be used to identify those people who became obstacles to U.S. expansion over the next century. Drinnon's "Red Man's Burden" posits the use of Indians as a way to maintain the defensive language necessary for imperialist gains. During the late-nineteenth and early-twentieth centuries American political and social discourse continued to exploit Indian imagery as a means of meeting the nation's ravenous appetite for territory and markets.

It is no surprise that the United States' brutal repression of the Filipino insurgency of 1899-1903 was conducted largely by officers and troopers who had recently participated in the Indian Wars of the Great Plains and in the American Southwest. The behavior of American soldiers in the Philippines manifested the national consensus attitude regarding U.S. policy in the region. Stuart Creighton Miller explains the correlation between the American mentality towards the Filipino frontier and its inhabitants,

> Proponents of expansion had hailed the islands as America's 'new frontier,' and appropriately enough, the men who conquered the Philippines, particularly the volunteers, brought with them a frontier spirit.... Virtually every member of the high command had spent most of his career terrorizing Apaches, Comanches, Kiowas, and the Sioux. Some had taken part in the massacre at Wounded Knee. It was easy for such commanders to order similar tactics in the Philippines.... And the men in their command, many of whom were themselves descendants of the old Indian fighters, carried out these orders with amazing, if not surprising, alacrity.[44]

The Indian-hating feature of America's racist ideology was passed on to a new Indian, and it is the Native American's "burden" to have their identity misappropriated for the United States' imperialist ventures into yet to be Americanized regions.

It was at this precise period, when the United States was entering into its overseas phase of imperialism, that cinema became an alternate means of influencing popular opinion. Examining late-nineteenth century literature to explain the rationale behind U.S. imperialism, historian Amy Kaplan insists that the American adventure in the Philippines and Cuba provided the perfect visual images to transfix an audience at a moment in the nation's history when American imperialist aggression was being hotly debated. The Spanish-American War and the development of cinema proved a perfect match.

As the hectic movement of troops preparing for battle helped gain the audience's undivided attention, cinema also became a conduit for political propaganda dissemination to the masses. On one level, the image of American troops engaging in overseas wars of conquest entertained the audience, on a secondary, and more discreet, plane the war films portrayed the American soldiers as vigorous and energetic representatives of the Anglo-Saxon Protestant people whose duty it was to regenerate the world and lift the "barbarous" peoples. During the first two decades of the twentieth century the transition from literature to film as the principal manner of engaging in a social discourse/allegory while entertaining the audience was in full development.

When media moguls discovered the mass marketing power of cinema during the 1910s the medium became the next logical stage in the development of the mechanisms for disseminating the national propaganda of U. S. expansionism. Although literary works such as Owen Wister's, *The Virginian* (1902), and Edgar Rice Burroughs, *Under the Moons of Mars* (1911), continued the traditional class and race allegory, cinema became a vital tool to the discipline during a time when racial discrimination intensified. The rich visual impact the medium offered its novice audience influenced the dramatic success of cinema over literature.

American cinema had its origins in an age when positivist-influenced race theories predominated social thought. Social Darwinism helped generate a racial hierarchy placing Anglo-Saxons above all the races. At the same time, Madison Grant was writing his elegy to the great white lineage, *The Passing of the Great Race* (1916). At the same time the goal of the pseudo-scientific eugenics movement to generate the perfect race had considerable academic legitimacy.

Although a few years away from reaching its apex of national support, the Ku Klux Klan, under the new direction of William Simmons, was reorganizing as the group planned its resurrection. It is little wonder one of this country's most influential cinematic masterpieces, D.W. Griffith's *The Birth of a Nation* (1915), depicts such a biased image of Reconstruction era Blacks.

President Woodrow Wilson described the film as the most accurate narrative of Reconstruction. The film exposed the nation's failed attempt at Black empowerment, and its tragic consequences upon the White South: "It is like writing history with Lightning," Wilson said, "and my only regret is that it is all so terribly true."[45] Wilson's heartfelt endorsement was a manifestation of the White nation's general abhorrence of the "Blacks," which in turn, illuminates the contemporary views on race that will also affect the image of Natives. Griffith's climactic rescue scene has the Ku Klux Klan riding into the town to save the embattled white woman from the beast-like Black soldiers. Richard Slotkin argues that, "[t]he visualization of that rescue as a struggle between men of White and Dark races for the body of a White woman is of course a fundamental trope of the Frontier myth."[46] *The Birth of a Nation* offered Griffith, like intellectuals and scholars of previous generations, the artistic canvas to express the social conscience of the age.

Despite the best efforts of Griffith apologists to refute any deliberate racism against Blacks in *The Birth of a Nation*,[47] the question of his negative depiction of Blacks remains trivial, to the more important question of the influence society played in his desire to portray Blacks so harshly. The more important factor scholars need understand from *The Birth of a Nation,* directly relates to historian of imperialism Frank Tucker's White Conscience,[48] that ideology that contributes to the audience's acceptance of the vulgar misrepresentations. Griffith was a racist because he was a man of his time, and the scholars, writers and politicians and popular White opinion of his time taught him Blacks and the "other" were evil inferior creatures, seeking to destroy the noble Anglo-Saxon American civilization. It is this deceptive ideology, now developing into a White (sub)Conscience, Americans have internalized, contributing to the tacit acceptance of racist behavior. Americans have experienced a collective schizophrenic episode, inherited from their European ancestors, seeking to simultaneously affirm and suppress the national identity. Thus, Americans will exalt and revel in the profits earned through time, while refuting the cost incurred.

According to Tucker's argument, America's failure to accept responsibility for the wretched conditions of the "other" is another manifestation of the White Conscience. It is replete with all the denials and rationale explaining the pitiful existence of the "other." Tucker identifies the single-most important factor influencing American concepts of non-Whites; as the justification of the economic exploitation of Brown people. While Tucker's argument still holds true, the nature of changing social movements has forced Americans to re-think this logic. Already influenced by the White Conscience and its colonizer language, Contemporary Anglo American view of race must deflect more effectively any criticism of exploitative behavior against people of color.

In 1967, as the White civil rights backlash rhetoric of Barry Goldwater and George Wallace was disseminating amongst disgruntled Americans, Tucker's White Conscience identified the aforementioned crucial element in the highly unbalanced American social structure. The exploitation of people of color was at the heart of the need to enact legislation to create an equal and just America. However, nearly four decades later the White Conscience fails to explain the survival of the most essential principles contributing to the exploitation of people of color. Conservative American factions have been especially successful in denouncing a key tool from the Civil Rights era, affirmative action. Claiming affirmative action has outlived its purpose Americans are convinced to eliminate this security net for people of color and women that defends them against the "old boy's network" institutionalized in American networks over the course of two centuries of privilege. The genesis and nourishment of an ideology that labels people of color as inferior validates White people's aggressive actions is firmly rooted in the continued existence of racialized principles post-Civil Rights Americans deny still survive. As the essence of Tucker's White Conscience becomes an artifact within the field of race theory, neo-colonialist discourse, or world globalization debate, the ideology survives within the subliminal mind of mainstream America.

As Americans watch on television news U.S. wars against Moslem people, debates over Indian gaming, or stories of young African American teens being sent to prison for having sex with White teens, they can find comfort in the knowledge that race does not influence any of these stories. The White (sub)Conscience explains how Americans can maintain the most fundamental racist qualities the White Conscience identifies, yet deny their own racist behavior. As literature, film, and later television all incorporated some feature of the White (sub)Conscience as part of its dialectic voice, one must separate and identify how the use of this exploitative ideology to understand the success it has in excusing a nation of its racist past, and more important, racist present.

Although the racist ideology slithered along its historical course, very little scholarly energy was spent on investigating the topic. The first significant studies of the ideology contributing to the oppression of the "other" only occurred after World War II when wars of liberation began popping up throughout the Third World.

Frantz Fanon and Albert Memmi set the standards by which the post-colonialist theorists measure themselves. Although these scholars express a discourse in their works critiquing political, economic, and social issues, these anti-colonialist arguments find a legitimate application towards understanding Hollywood's depiction of Indians in cinema. During the height of the colonialist wars of liberation during the 1950s and 1960s, scholars sought to explain the perplexing behavior of so many people of color who resented benevolent European rule. Anti-colonialist scholars explained the conscious effort of the White man to make race the fundamental factor shaping relations between the European colonizers and the colonized Natives. In turn, descendents of this colonizer society re-defined the ideological rampart thwarting any criticism resulting from the exploitation of the Natives.[49]

The fundamental underpinning in any study of colonialism is White people's denial of any wrongdoing towards the people of color they are abusing. Layer upon layer of repudiations and accusations against the colonized shield Whites from blame. American culture has employed the traditional European deflective means that additionally serve to place all blame on the victims of colonialism. The sanctioning of anti-colored propaganda camouflaged as popular culture entertainment, especially film, has given Americans a conscience-cleansing mechanism to continue with their productive lives absolved of any guilt for the nation's ridiculously high standard of living (in comparison to the nations providing the resources generating the United States' lifestyle). Despite the best interests of liberal reformers, however, White Americans cannot separate their comfortable life from the dire straits of the oppressed they claim to assist. According to the Tunisian born philosopher, Albert Memmi, that the alleged reformers directly benefit from the colonizer/colonized relationship is sufficient to obscure a legitimate reason to eliminate the bond.[50] Rather than change the situation reformers in fact, seek to rewrite history in such a way as to deny the colonized any reputable role in the development of the region in question.[51] In the case of Native Americans, the denial takes on the effect of placing Natives outside of the civilized world as "savages," thus insuring the need to "save" the backward Indian.

Fanon further insists that the colonial world is a Manichean world; a place where the colonizer describes the native as the "quintessence of evil."[52] As colonizers stripped their colonies of natural resources to lift their own standard of living, the White European colonist identified Natives as a people devoid of any civilized characteristics, and this justified their oppression and exploitation. As if engaged in a social discourse with his/her own conscience, the White colonizer ceaselessly uses the image of the colonized as a means for washing the blood from his/her hands. Memmi explains that the colonizer is aware of his/her privileged, illegitimate status. Understanding that there were other colonialists usurping Native sovereignty deflected guilt from one's own exploitative behavior.[53] The repression of guilt contributes to the White Conscience's "willful veiling of reality"[54] and the invention of a "truth" about people of color warranting the intervention of the colonialist White.

The two most persistent elements in the "White Myth" are the institutionalization of a racial hierarchy between Whites and people of color and a denial by Whites that creating such a social order is a moral transgression. Each belief nourishes the other, and without the other each succumbs to the truth. Tucker explains, "[t]he evils of racism seem to thrive best when the guilty nation does not recognize the evil."[55] Thus, according to Tucker, the key element in maintaining racial superiority is to deny the existence of racism.

White Culture refuses to accept responsibilities for its actions by denying the existence of a problem.

The literary history of the United States has had a steady dose of this White Conscience ideology. By the (mis)appropriation of Indian imagery, American clergymen, writers, and political leaders have felt the pulse of the nation and shaped its social consciousness. To reiterate Louis Owen's argument, there is no "real" Indian. The only Indian that exists lives in the guilt-riddled colonizer fantasy world that is the American psyche. In this colonizer-mentality world Americans use the Indian image to convince themselves that their hostile and abusive actions towards Natives are warranted because of imminent physical threats the latter pose to Americans, or the failure of the Indians to recognize the inherent value of "civilization" and the democratic principles associated with progress. During the initial stages of the twentieth century, cinema became an eager and willing accomplice in developing narratives both to entertain and indoctrinate an audience for the purpose of sustaining the national ideology of racial and cultural subjugation.

During the silent era, when D. W. Griffith's *The Birth of a Nation* was proving the entertainment value of cinema, films employed Indians as they had appeared in American literature for generations, either as the heartless savage or as the noble subordinate, ready to sacrifice his/her life to rescue the inherently superior white character. Such was the case in Griffith's own, *Iola's Promise* (1912), when white Mary Pickford's Indian maiden, Iola, forfeits her life to her own tribe in order to save the family of the white man who earlier had rescued her, and showed kindness as he treated the wounds she received at the hands of evil whites.[56] A similar theme incorporating the doomed Indian is George Seitz's The *Vanishing American* (1925), where a reference to Herbert Spencer's survival of the fittest introduced the film. As the Indian hero, Nophaie, whose

68

love for the white teacher, Marion, goes unreciprocated, dies attempting to bring peace, he once again postulates the superiority of the Whites over the noble red man.[57] Although the plight of the Indian was portrayed sympathetically, the metaphoric claim focuses on racial and cultural primacy— in this case, white supremacy. Silent era films reminded the viewer, whether the Indian was noble and just, or a devious savage, nature doomed him to oblivion.

The silent film era acted as the transitional mechanism that took the literary social message from the mass marketed plays, novels, novellas, and dime novels into the visually rich medium of cinema. The silent film demonstrated that it was viable moneymaking commodity, and as was the case with stage and literature, the social discourse of the day was woven into the story the filmmakers presented. This visual social narrative incorporated the same literary principles to tell its story that writers of generations before had done. Influenced by decades of American literary theories and constructs, filmmakers applied the same standards to their work. Amongst the oldest and most revered American storytelling techniques was the Indian as national metaphor. Unable to come up with anything more original than their literary predecessors, or perhaps, firm believers in the White (sub)Conscience ideology, filmmakers continued to use Indians as a dual figure— both as entertainment and as social allegory.

Raised during the golden age of television, my social conscience was influenced by the western "talkies," the "cowboys and Indians" films produced during the height of the genre's popularity, 1930s through the 1960s. Silent film westerns established the genre as a viable product, but it was the sound versions that appeared as reruns on television. Growing up in southern California during the Sixties, it was these movies that I saw countless times on weekday afternoons on KNXT's "Early Show," occasionally on weeknights on KHJ's "Million Dollar Movie," or its Saturday afternoon cinematic bill of fare "Adventure Theater." Regardless of the time or day, they are the movies that gave me my indoctrination into the world of Native Americans and their role in the development of the United States. It was these film Indians that became my source of reference for American Indians. Surrounded by a world of indigenous customs and behaviors in my own home, not surprisingly, it was these television Indians that taught me about "real Indians." These were my childhood Indians, the very same images that were to influence my generation of Americans as to the legitimacy of our indigenous ancestors.

The images of Indians have been redefined over the course of the past century to meet the socio-political question of the time, yet "Indians" as a construct continue to be the exclusive property of mainstream America's social conscience. Whether their image has been appropriated to depict the racialized savage beasts of the colonizer's mind, or the paternalistic dependent children of the sympathetic reformer, the Indian that exists in our society is a character meant to soothe the national consciousness. That conscience must somehow come to grips with five hundred years of social and cultural genocide of indigenous people. As Louis Owens has argued, there is a perverse national obsession with Indians that seeks simultaneously to desire and destroy them.[58] This sentiment is directly related to the colonizer mentality that is a major feature in the White (sub)Conscience, a social conscience that is highly visible in the Childhood Indian films I, and many from my generation, considered authentic depictions of the West and its players. These are the images that would guide a generation of gullible viewers, and beyond, to understand the unreciprocated father/child relationship existing between the federal government and Native Americans. Each and every question a young child has

70

about Indians can be easily understood in the context of the western films "authentic" depiction of the West. It is in the western genre films that Americans are best able to understand their detestable use of Indian imagery as a (mis)appropriated socio-political tool employed to defend the virtues of the White (sub)Conscience-motivated "American Dream." A close examination of a cross-section of westerns will expose the practice of Indian image (mis)appropriation in cinema as a behavior that has been part of American society since the colonial era and helps the nation cope with its colonizer origins and deny its continued racism. The manner in which Indians are portrayed in cinema will change over the course of time, but, the reason they appear in a film are as old as Mary Rowlandson's escape narrative, or Pocahontas' love story on an American stage. They help forge the American national identity; an identity most Americans do not know (or perhaps, are just unwilling to admit) is rich in white supremacist tradition.

ENDNOTES CHAPTER 2

[1] David Theo Goldberg, *Racist Culture: Philosophy and the Politics of Meaning*, Oxford: Blackwell Publishing, (1993), 1.

[2] Goldberg, *Racist Culture*, iii.

[3] Goldberg, *Racist Culture*, 6.

[4] Frantz Fanon, translated by Constance Farrington, *The Wretched of the Earth*, New York: Grove Press, (1963), 7.

[5] The context of Disraeli's actual statement reads, " A Saxon race, protected by an insular position, has stamped its diligent and methodic character on the century. And when a superior race, with a superior idea to work and order, advances, its state will be progressive.... All is race; there is no other truth." *Tancred*, (1847).

[6] Goldberg, *Racist Culture*, 6.

[7] John Carlos Rowe, *Literary Culture and U.S. Imperialism: From the Revolution to World War II*, Oxford: Oxford University Press, (2000), xi.

[8] Robert Berkhofer Jr., *The White Man's Indian*, New York: Vintage Books, (1978), 28.

[9] Robert Berkhofer, xiii.

[10] See "Beads and Buckskin: Reading Authenticity in Native American Literature" in Louis Owens's, *Mixed Messages: Literature, Film, Family, Place*, Norman: University of Oklahoma Press, (1998).

[11] Although it is true that early colonizers of the "New World" used religion to distinguish "otherness," the success of colonialism by White Christian nations amongst people of color will eventually contribute to the racialized discourse in the nineteenth century necessary to differentiate between the colonizer and the colonized. Racism became the lynchpin in defense of nineteenth century colonialism. Regardless of the three-century lag in racist ideology, Columbus' "discovery" will contribute to the development of racist discourse in the nineteenth century.

[12] Richard Slotkin, *Regeneration Through Violence*, Middletown, Connecticut: Wesleyan University Press, (1973), 83-84.

[13] Berkhofer, 80-85.

[14] Slotkin, *Regeneration Through Violence*, 102-103.

[15] Slotkin, *Regeneration Through Violence*, 154.

[16] Richard Drinnon, *Facing West*, New York: Schocken Books, (1990) c1980, 67.

[17] Vine Deloria, Jr., *God is Red*, New York: Dell Publishing Company, (1973), 127.

[18] Philip J. Deloria, *Playing Indian*, New Haven: Yale University Press, (1998), 21-22.

[19] Philip J. Deloria, 69.

[20] For a provocative and insightful examination of the paradoxical goals of Indian sovereignty the fledgling United States faced during this period as a result of western settler's ambitions pertaining to Indian lands, see Patrick Griffin's *American Leviathan: Empire,*

Nation, and Revolutionary Frontier, Hill and Wang, (2007).

[21] Bernard W. Sheehan, *Seeds of Extinction: Jeffersonian Philanthropy and the American Indian*, New York: W.W. Norton & Company, (1973), 110-111.

[22] Drinnon, 81-82.

[23] Drinnon, 82.

[24] Drinnon, 84-85.

[25] Susan Scheckel, *The Insistence of the Indian: Race and Nationalism in Nineteenth-Century American Culture*, Princeton: Princeton University Press, (1998), 7.

[26] Reginald Horsman, *Race and Manifest Destiny: The Origins of American Racial Anglo-Saxonism*, Cambridge: Harvard University Press, (1981), 112-114.

[27] Horsman, 114.

[28] Slotkin, *Regeneration Through Violence*, 274.

[29] Slotkin, *Regeneration Through* Violence, 275.

[30] Slotkin, *Regeneration Through Violence*, 466-467.

[31] Scheckel, 15.

[32] Slotkin, 491.

[33] Scheckel, 48.

[34] Rowe, 55.

[35] Rowe, 55 and 60.

[36] Horsman, 123.

[37] Rowe, 61.

[38] Rowe, 64.

[39] Rowe, 64-65.

[40] Richard Slotkin, *The Fatal Environment*, Middletown, Connecticut: Wesleyan University Press, (1985), 117.

[41] Slotkin, *The Fatal Environment*, 364.

[42] Nell Irving Painter, *Standing at Armageddon: The United States, 1877-1919*, New York: W.W. Norton & Company, (1987), 26-27.

[43] Richard Drinnon, "Red Man's Burden," *Inquiry*, I (June 26, 1978), 20-22.

[44] Stuart Creighton Miller, *Benevolent Assimilation: The American Conquest of the Philippines, 1899-1903*, New Haven: Yale University Press, (1982), 195.

[45] Richard Slotkin, *Gunfighter Nation*, Norman: University of Oklahoma Press, (1992), 240.

[46] Slotkin, *Gunfighter Nation*, 241.

[47] Clyde Taylor, "The Re-Birth of the Aesthetic in Cinema," *The Birth of Whiteness*, edited by Daniel Bernardi, New Brunswick, New Jersey: Rutgers University Press, (1996), 18-19.

[48] Frank H. Tucker, *The White Conscience*, New York: Frederick Unger Publishing Co., (1968), 9-15.

75

[49] During the past decade there has been an increase of scholars re-examining the colonialist mentality and applying a more contemporary reading. Of special interest to the Native American theme is the late Louis Owens' *Mixed Blood Messages* (1998). In a related field, race theoretician David Theo Goldberg has led a strong field of scholars studying race issues. The work of these scholars provides strong evidence that the academic world is confronting the source of the racially motivated oppression of Brown people.

[50] Albert Memmi, *The Colonizer and the Colonized*, London: Earthscan Publications, (1990) c1965, 70-84.

[51] Fanon, *The Wretched of the Earth*, 51.

[52] Fanon, *The Wretched of the Earth*, 41.

[53] Memmi, 9.

[54] Tucker, 11.

[55] Ibid.

[56] Michael Hilger, *From Savages to Nobleman*, Lanham, Md.: Scarecrow Press, Inc., (1995), 18-19.

[57] Jacquelyn Kilpatrick, *Celluloid Indians*, Lincoln: University of Nebraska Press, (1999), 29-33.

[58] Owens, 117.

Chapter 3
Holding the Fort:Early Cinematic Indian Images
Maintain the Colonizer Mentality
Of the National Myth.

By the time the early twentieth century's silent film era came to an end, Hollywood was well indoctrinated in the principles of the White (sub)Conscience. For over two centuries an aggressive, expansionist America had incorporated into its myth-making apparatus written material about Native Americans passed off as popular entertainment. It was the motion picture industry's turn to affect the nation's social conscience and justifying the exploitation of Natives. Regarding the film industry's role in reproducing the national myth and subsequent function of Natives in the master narrative, the first two phases of Indian film imagery maintained negative to extremely negative stereotypes. As silent films became part of the mainstream culture, the motion picture industry demonstrated proficiency for depicting Natives in the stereotypical demeaning images that intellectuals, politicians, the clergy, and entertainers had used for generations to argue and sustain the social, cultural, or racial superiority of the American people.

Over the course of the past century, cinema and television have become America's primary entertainment and communication apparatus. The significance in this change from a print media to a visual source is directly related to the strength of visual imagery. Film historian Ray B. Browne posits that motion pictures carry messages with much more lucidity than does the written word. The aesthetic power of film brings to life essential factors in developing the story. The artistic power of the film seduces the viewer to accept the film's messages, whether they are truths or lies, and although words do the same, the mass media appeal of films, along with its vibrant images produce a more effective message than does the written word.[1]

This factor has a major consequence on the manner in which Americans experience the changing dynamics of social and political moods, for film historian Peter C. Rollins argues that Hollywood has inadvertently chronicled the nation's changing frame of mind. As the national mood changes filmmakers record on film society's mores and values, thus Americans see themselves on the screen regardless of the setting.[2] Film historian Peter Biskind argues that while producer, director and writer may have conflicting cinematic goals, the resulting film is a manifestation of society's ideology: the films both influence and reflect manners, attitudes, and behavior. Most importantly, although the viewer is unaware of the message, he/she tends to accept the context the film furnishes.[3]

It is this continuous nationally institutionalized mis-representation of American Indians that allows the country to purge itself of any collective guilt resulting from the abuses of Natives. In film the Indian maintains its place as a primitive creature of nature. Locked in the nineteenth century national imagery vault, and depicted as bloodthirsty savage, noble chief, lustful squaw or trustworthy sidekick the Native remains inferior to, and dependent on, the more acculturated and civilized Whites. Once again the rationale behind the exploitative and inaccurate depiction of Natives slithers back to the paternalistic feature of the White (sub)Conscience. This element of the White sub(Conscience) is a critical component in film scripts.

Due to the time constraint involved in developing a story in a film or television program, the industry places a premium on symbolism, rather than realism.[4] Whether done intentionally or not, film characters are not representative of its viewing audience; they are figurative images expressing preferred cultural attitudes and mores, the most visible of these symbolic portrayals center on power relations, and the relative value of culture.[5] This in turn translates into the establishment of a national social status in which the characters viewed as having strong television and film images are seen as being the most dependable in real life. In contrast, those groups seen less often in these roles are held in lesser esteem.[6]

There is little surprise that in my "Childhood Indian" films, the White male appeared most often in the strong character roles, while the Natives played perfunctory parts secondary to the White hero. The inability of viewers to distinguish between make-believe and reality hinders society's capacity to exercise a fair perception of the world they live in. Althea C. Huston, an expert on television's effect on children, explains, "Even when people recognize that the material they are viewing is fictional, its message and images gradually shape expectations and beliefs about this real world."[7] This context sustained the "center of power" and "culture value" Huston argues played such a significant role on television during the 1960s and '70s. Even as the Civil Rights Movement is battling for the equality of color and gender, viewers still see White men as the symbolic role model in American society.

In a culture dominated by a White (sub)Conscience, Natives must battle against discriminatory ideals the offenders may not even be aware they are displaying. It is from this negative perception; reinforced by film, that Americans pre-determine the social position Natives must begin their ascent into social respectability. Afflicted by the public propaganda replete with all the racialized terminology shaping the mental image society developed about Natives, including their physical, psychological, and cultural attributes, Native Americans face a disturbingly difficult task fitting into mainstream America's concept of the ideal citizen, while trying to maintain their own cultural identity.

Talking films carried on the ideas and concepts of American superiority with little change, the

White (sub)Conscience was alive and well. Within the context of this work the White (sub)Conscience appears in the film depiction of Natives in two traditional theoretical threads, the colonizer mentality and the paternalistic. A third, and more contemporary feature, places negative Indian imagery in period works that express the attitudes of the film's time on politics and social issues, such as the Cold War, the Civil Rights, or the Vietnam War.

Historian John A. Price claims that the development of Indian images occurred over three phases. The first two phases cover from the silent era up to the beginning of the Cold War (1908-29 and 1930-1947), and are recognized for their negative to extremely negative portrayal of Indian images.[8] Those negative portrayals are directly related to the colonizer mentality reflective of a society imbued with the racist rationale of a people fresh from a century of conquests of people of color in the American west, Mexico, Central America, the Philippines, and China. American racial attitudes during these decades gave Hollywood little reason to depict people of color in any manner that could challenge the racial or cultural superiority of the White Anglo-Saxon American.

The popularity of westerns during the 1930s secured a place for Native Americans in film, unfortunately the images are shaped by the socially acceptable ideas and mores of the era. The White (sub)Conscience secured American concepts of cultural and racial superiority. This unconscious racialized social perception gave Americans the freedom to maintain racist beliefs without feeling guilty for their principles, while also sustaining white supremacist attitudes in the national discourse. The Indian image in film during this generation was greatly influenced by this colonizer mentality. Fully indoctrinated into White (sub)Conscience, the film industry employed negative imagery of Natives as a universal concept. Hollywood portrayed its Indians in the socially comfortable colonizer images Americans had come to accept as normal.

This chapter will analyze the colonized image of Natives in film and television that American society came to see as representing "real" Indians. In these films Hollywood depicts Natives using the most standard literary images. These are the same visual characterizations of Natives that prior generations of Americans were raised on in literature and silent era cinema. Indians were caricature figures that allowed for the frontier-based story to develop the heroic exploits of Hollywood's white male protagonist. Sprinkled into the narrative, perhaps unconsciously, but most assuredly affected by the White (sub)Conscience, were subtle, and not so subtle reminders of American cultural and racial superiority.

As a child growing up in the 1960s when the westerns dominated Los Angeles television, there was never a dearth of Saturday afternoon "cowboys and Indians" movies to keep this impressionable young boy entertained. After the movies ended this same boy quickly sped out to his backyard and played his own version of the "winning of the west." That his two grandmothers held strong indigenous traditions and gave daily lessons on Native beliefs and practices was irrelevant. His imagination carried him off to foreboding encounters with bloodthirsty savages who had little respect for the principles of human decency. These imaginary Indians were the same merciless creatures depicted in those Saturday afternoon westerns. These were the Indians Americans were taught to fear. Their sole purpose for existence was to terrorize civilized people whose only crime was their strong appreciation of freedom, individualism, and progress, things the "Indians" could never fully understand.

This Indian image is the foundation of the colonizer mentality scholars such as Frantz Fanon

81

and Albert Memmi identified in their classic studies of colonialism. The fear of the Natives is a key tool the colonizer employs to defend their abusive and exploitative behavior towards the colonized. Although Memmi identifies the colonizer's self-denial as the critical component in colonialism,[9] recent cultural studies and race theory scholarship has given more credibility to his argument. The continuing debate recent scholars have maintained over the level of racism still present in society sustains the existence of the White (sub)Conscience, the national social myth that helps to explain American aggressive and exploitative behavior towards people of color.

Recent race and neo-colonialist scholarship identify the common denominator of Native threats to the White community's safety as reason enough to eradicate people of color. Edward Said's landmark study, *Orientalism* (1978), identifies fear of Arab customs as a motivating factor contributing to the negative stereotypes Western society uses to identify the former.[10] Richard Drinnon explains in his book *Facing West* (1990) the metaphysics of Indian-hating as a key feature in the United States' western expansion, and subsequent imperialist adventures abroad. According to Drinnon, this Indian-hating is justified by the fears of alleged Indian belligerence towards Whites.[11] Richard Slotkin devotes three extensively researched volumes of scholarship to explaining United States aggression against people of color.[12] Slotkin's "Myth of the Frontier" theme is fueled significantly by a fear of the "Other." More recently, Amy Kaplan's *The Anarchy of Empire in the Making of U.S. Culture* (2002), argues U.S. imperialist expansion was a response to the fears of political and social anarchy in places such as Hawaii and the Philippines.[13]

These are but a small cross-section of the various monographs explaining how policies of aggression have been metamorphosed into a mechanism of self-preservation. It is the Native's belligerent behavior that warrants such extreme levels of American brutality against Natives. What these scholars, and their contemporaries, have failed to explain is how American society has internalized this fear so deeply in its social conscience that it has become incapable of distinguishing fact from fiction when dealing with Natives. In fact, in American society the fiction has become the fact. As part of the White (sub)Conscience, the fear of the Native has assisted in generating the national image of a people (Natives) devoid of human qualities. To earlier generations of Americans, Indians were the human sharks inhabiting the open seas of the American frontier searching for their next victim. Without missing a beat, Hollywood incorporated this image into the narratives of its first generation of post-silent era westerns.

These westerns had remarkable staying power, due to television. Three decades later, these very same westerns influenced a new generation of Americans' understanding of Indian images. Even as the civil rights movement was at its apex and the nation sought to end racism, Saturday afternoon television was showing a new generation of Americans the old racist depiction of Native Americans earlier generations had accepted as authentic. The White (sub)Conscience ideology ensured that this new generation also accepted these images as reality. These are the "Childhood Indians" of the baby-boomers, and as they grew up the Indian images of their parents and grand parents became theirs.

These films maintained the racialized imagery of the Native critical to the American meta-narrative, a story predicated on White Supremacy. As race theoretician David Theo Goldberg argues, "Sewn over the centuries into the seams of the social fabric, the idea of race…" becomes the basis by which complex social emotions are articulated.[14] Amongst these emotions are fear and anxieties. As Fanon and Memmi theorized colonialism, the shared fears and anxieties a society felt are a result of the guilt that arises from their knowledge that their (colonizer) wealth and power is a consequence of the Natives' exploited condition. In the case of the United States, Indians become the iconography for a national repudiation of racist behavior.

According to Drinnon, racial oppression has critical consequences for the American identity. "Anchored however obscurely in the unconscious," Drinnon argues, "it became a key component of the national theology, from the Bay Colony's New Israel to the republic's Manifest Destiny and the white man's burden and New Frontier."[15] These consequences will result in the socially acceptable concept of dark-skinned "others" posing a threat to the advance of the American wave of progress. Herman Melville's "Metaphysics of Indian-hating" becomes the American response to the fears and anxieties called forth by the Native presence. In the twentieth century the racist depictions of Natives in silent era and early sound films are a manifestation of socially implicit concepts rooted in trepidation and revulsion. Developed through popular culture and public discourse, Americans came to accept as "fact" the negative imagery of Indians without question. To mainstream Americans, it was just "how it is."

To fully understand the role of racism within the context of the White (sub)Conscience ideology, one must first examine the features of colonizer mentality that identifies the "bloodthirsty" behavior of Indians. The Indian's behavior is irrational and thus requires the brutal, but necessary, response of the American figures. It is in the pre-World War II talking films that this representation flourished and generated the most comprehensive cross-section of cinematic negative Indian imagery. When sound films made their introduction the racialized, colonizer-influenced, images of Indians were the conventional depiction American audiences came to know as the "authentic" Indian. This matter-of-fact Indian image sustained the commonly held concept of a white supremacist America capable of overcoming any human obstacle, regardless of color.[16] Regardless of the film genre Indians survived the transition into sound and were easily integrated into 1930s narratives and subplots.

The 1930s witnessed a successful run of horror films that built up the tension of perceived and unseen terror. Drawing from this very successful genre, in his epic western *Stagecoach* (1939), John Ford creates the horror film tension with the foreboding threat of an Apache attack on the helpless stagecoach; helping to keep the audience on the edge of its seat. The passengers in the stagecoach represented a cross-section of the American public character that faced the dangers of the unknown. Ford made no attempts to camouflage their symbolic purpose in the film. Slotkin explains, "...Ford's deliberate play with type-casting categories is a way of invoking the memories that such movie-stereotypes contain, the framework of associations with earlier stories that defines each character's meaning and mode of action."[17]

Riding shotgun and protecting the passengers from attack was the hard-nosed, but kind-hearted town marshal, Curly, symbolic of an American legal system that was firm, but just. Amongst the passengers is the embezzling banker, representative of the callous industrialist who selfishly cared only about his own personal gains. The pregnant wife who is traveling to be with her husband, who himself is defending the frontier against the savage obstructing progress, identifies the loyal woman who will follow her husband and battle the wilderness as a family. There is also the milquetoast traveling salesman who, despite his frail appearance, ventured out into the wilderness: it is safe to say that even the weakest American will test his mettle against the dreaded unknown. Also making up the passenger list are the reluctant, and as we discover during the story somewhat naïve, outlaw, Ringo Kid, played so brilliantly by John Wayne, and his prostitute "with the heart of gold" love interest, Dallas. Both characters overcome their shady past to find a future on the frontier.

On the stagecoach's journey to Lordsburg the passengers' interaction is influenced by the dark, ominous threat of the unseen, but menacing Apache horde. Like the mythographic characterization of the *Stagecoach* passengers, the Apaches also have their symbolic role to play, in their case, as a "menacing abstraction"[18] of evil. As Slotkin argues, Ford's *Stagecoach* characters were transparent stereotypes the audience was meant to identify with. The Indian images from *Stagecoach* were offered with the same intention, although within the context of the White (sub)Conscience ideology. Reminiscent of the horror film genre popular at the time the Apaches played the concealed beast that was waiting to pounce on its unsuspecting victim. American audiences had little trouble identifying the Apaches as the hidden terror. Small effort on the part the public's imagination was necessary to perceive the unseen Indian as the threatening hidden creature. This sentiment was already deeply embedded in the national psyche.

Ford's Indian maintained its place in the national mythology as the menace to civilization. The fortuitous arrival of the United States Cavalry during the climactic chase not only saved the passengers, especially the women, from a certain "fate worse than death,"[19] it reinforced the long-standing myth of White invincibility against the savage inhabitants of the frontier. Along with assisting in creating an essential backdrop for Ford's more critical storyline about relationships between the characters on the stagecoach, the Indians help sustained principles by which White America defended its privileged position of power.

This position includes the right to exterminate the Indian as if vermin. No film in the author's childhood better depicted this "truth" than King Vidor's 1940 abomination, *Northwest Passage*. In the film, Rogers' Rangers are an elite colonial New England militia specializing in Indian warfare and fighting on the British side during the Seven Years War. They are led by their commanding officer William Rogers, who in his own right is described by his men as a better Indian than the Indians.[20] Charged with avenging an Abenaki attack against British colonists, the Rangers embark on an epic, an endurance testing, and spirit-challenging journey deep into enemy territory.

During the build-up to the climactic battle, the Abenaki are described in the most distasteful of terms. In Fanonesque language the Abenaki represent "the absence of values." Their fate is sealed because they are heartless, demonic creatures, devoid of any human qualities. The Abenaki are contaminated with heathen customs, they are "the deforming element, defiguring (*sic*) all that has to do with beauty or morality; …the depository of maleficent powers"[21] and must be destroyed before they are able to strike against the vulnerable frontier settlers. In the context of a colonizer mentality the Abenaki must be made despicable, for the purpose of the Rangers' raid is to obliterate the village at Saint Francis in Quebec, Canada and its Indian inhabitants. Vidor depicts his Abenaki according to 1940s socially agreeable images of the deplorable, deceitful, and deadly American Indians. In *Northwest Passage* the Indians serve a critical component of the White (sub)Conscience. Despite their constant attacks on the American Spirit, and regardless of the dark depths to which these tests drive these national heroes, the Americans win—Americans always win.

In *Northwest Passage*, Indians act as mere props for the "real" story, and as soon as the narrative allowed they were removed from the film. Besides Rogers'

87

small unit of unknown tribal identity Indians, and of course, the Abenaki, the other Indians in the film, Iroquois (Mohawk), are the British allied, mind you British, not American, allies. Vidor removes this complicated element early in the film. Within a historical context the presence of the Iroquois provide Vidor a serious dilemma to depicting the story as an American tale of survival. During the colonial period the British, French, and the American colonist, for that matter, used local Natives in combat against their European foe or menacing Indian neighbors. In many of these situations it is the presence of the Native forces that help turn the tide of victory.

Ironically, one of the most significant examples of this result is the Mohawk presence during the King Philip's War, when they aided the colonist in the struggle against Metacom (King Philip) and his Wampanoag. When New York colony sent forces to reinforce its embattled Massachusetts neighbor, it also sent a large party of its Mohawk allies who proved the deciding factor defeating their political and economic indigenous rival.

In Vidor's story the Mohawk receive a far different interpretation. An incident where a keg of gunpowder is accidentally discharged causes Rogers to dismiss a large group of Iroquois warriors who were augmenting his small detachment of Rangers. Belittled and shamed by Rogers the Iroquois return to the British fort at Ticonderoga. The Iroquois in *Northwest Passage* are exposed as lackeys to the British, this characterization and the powder keg incident provide Vidor the perfect solution to a predicament requiring the sharing of heroic actions with Indians. Now Vidor can depict the story without the need to include Indians in the more complex narrative of survival against the elements by means of a superhuman effort by the frontier militia. In a White (sub)Conscience context, the heroes in *Northwest Passage* must be Americans—they must always be the hero.

However, it is the Rangers' attack upon the Abenaki village that is the most wretched example of the Indian imagery work Hollywood produced during the first two decades of sound films. As is the case with hundreds of films where Indians and whites do battle, the inept Indian warriors[24] fire wildly as the Rangers calmly pick out their targets. Even with all the confusion and smoke the white soldiers never kill one woman or child, and the Abenaki haphazardly run directly into the organized lines of the disciplined militia. After witnessing the slaughter of every single warrior (which appear to number in the hundreds) at Saint Francis without the Rangers killing any noncombatants, the viewer then sees the dozen or so women and children living in the village. Rogers gives the survivors a speech warning them he will do the same to any one else threatening the frontier. Vidor pays little attention to plight of the survivors, other than to act as a conduit for Rogers to remind (reassure) the audience of the brutal response Americans launches against its threats, in particular those coming from Natives.

It is doubtful any Americans truly want to know that the victims of a brilliant victory by their heroes retained any qualities that one could misconstrue as human. Albert Memmi long ago explained the significance of the dehumanization of the colonized in order to justify the superiority of the white colonizer. Even in film, Memmi's example of rules of colonizer conduct is respectfully adhered to. Cloaked in the guise of entertainment, the roots of the White (sub)Conscience stretch further into the bedrock of national thought. Cinema is supplementing the national indoctrination that American literature had steadfastly conducted until the more visually powerful film age arrived. Yet still the most delicate of tasks these mediums must tackle from generation to generation is the legitimizing of American

(White) rule over a land it has no moral or historical attachment to. Within this framework it becomes necessary to eliminate the Indian at all cost, for the Native is a constant reminder of the usurper status of the colonizer.[22] On screen, once the Indian has given the white hero the medium to show his superiority, the Indian must be erased in order to more fully develop the White characters in the story.

To further illuminate the interwoven relationship between cinema and the White (sub)Conscience, in 1940 the Department of Secondary Teachers of the National Education Association chose the film for study. The agency claimed, "Rogers comes to personify man's refusal to bow to the physical forces, and the success of this hardy band of early pioneers symbolizes our own struggle against bitter enemies in the modern world."[23] Jacquelyn Kilpatrick perceptively reminds her audience that she doubts Natives appreciated their ancestors being compared to Hitler and Mussolini's fascist threats in Europe.[24] Elaborating on Kilpatrick's point, to a 1940s America imbued with all the racialized language associated with its colonizer past, the sadistic description (The audience never actually witnesses Abenaki atrocities) of Abenaki behavior and the precision-like combat tactics of the white Rangers satisfies the white supremacist influenced polarized imagery of the two peoples.

In an age when the American people held openly racist imagery of people of color, *Northwest Passage*'s Abenakis sustain the colonizer concept of the White (sub)Conscience. By their savagery, they invited their own violent defeat. And American use of force to bring under submission such savage creatures devoid of human qualities that threaten the very existence of civilization is fully justified.

Following in the footsteps of *Northwest Passage* is Raoul Walsh's fictionalized account of George Armstrong Custer's military career, *They Died With*

90

Their Boots On (1942). During the 1930s it was Hollywood that brought to life the legacy of British colonialism in cinema favorites such as, *The Charge of the Light Brigade* (1936), *Wee Willie Winkie* (1937), and *Gunga Din* (1939).

The standard story in these films has the British official trying to negotiate a treaty with a deceitful, snake-like Native "khan" who betrays the trusting Englishmen. The loathsome khan and his henchmen, despite the element of surprise or overwhelming numbers, are no match for the resourceful Anglo-Saxon soldier however, who puts the defeated Natives back in their proper place. These Hollywood sagas are replete with the iconography of a traditional colonizer mentality: women and children endangered by Natives, dimwitted Natives holding little regard for human life, and Natives maintaining ritualistic cult-like superstitions, instead of "real" religion. All support the colonizer image of Natives Fanon and Memmi identify and critique in their works.

The fast-paced, action-filled, adventure film provides the opportunity for the enigmatic actor Errol Flynn to display his swashbuckling charm in an American version of the colonial war genre popular at the time. *They Died With Their Boots On* gave American audiences a look at colonial era wars of conquest with an American hero: George Armstrong Custer, albeit portrayed by a British actor. Although the first half of *They Died With Their Boots On* depicts Custer's Civil War exploits, the second half of the film provides director Raoul Walsh his canvas to paint the picture of physical and moral superiority of the Anglo-Saxon over the Native, as per the colonizer mentality.

Two separate incidents in the film illustrate these very points. As he arrives in Dakota Territory (which looks more like eastern California's Owens Valley, where it was filmed than the plains ecosystem of Montana and the Dakotas)[26] Custer catches a glimpse of a noble warrior, who is soon identified as Crazy Horse, Custer's primary Indian rival, who maneuvers his horse in and around the poorly trained American cavalry. It is Custer who eventually brings down the Indian. In his first encounter with his Red rival, George Armstrong Custer (Errol Flynn) defeats the Sioux war chief, Crazy Horse (Anthony Quinn), in a one on one duel. Suffice to say, the Sioux's best warrior was no match for Custer.[27] Little is left to the viewer's imagination. Custer's defeat of Crazy Horse expressed the publicly acceptable position of the physically superior Anglo-Saxon race. Even more symbolic of virtuous Anglo-Saxon justice is Custer's decision to arrest Crazy Horse, rather than kill him on the spot.[28] When Crazy Horse is rescued from the fort's stockade[29] by an Indian trading at the fort, Custer is in awe of the warrior's acrobatic riding skills and quickly embarks on a training program for his men to defeat this gallant foe.

Only after Custer instills an esprit-de-corps into his troopers with the old Irish pub song "Garry Owens" is his 7th Cavalry ready to do battle with Crazy Horse's Sioux. Having spent so long on the frontier, like the adventurers of American frontier myth Slotkin discusses who prepared the land for settlement, but were consumed by nature's siren's song, no longer suitable to live amongst civilized Man, Custer will re-instill into his men the élan that identifies them as agents of American civilization. It is an English gentleman he met during the Civil War who introduces him to the song that soon becomes the brigade's theme song. Thus, a tune from an occupied land of the British Empire helps remind Custer's 7th Cavalry of their colonialist legacy and their responsibility to perform as representatives of their nation (race).[30] With their pride restored the 7th Cavalry will help Custer serve his nation in a most gallant gesture.

The second significant symbolic incident occurs when Custer and his 7th Cavalry are defeated at the

Battle of the Little Big Horn. Hollywood uses creative license to turn an ignominious defeat by U.S. forces at the hands of Natives into a gallant display of American morality. According to the film, Custer decided to sacrifice himself, and his nearly three hundred men, to expose the corruption plaguing the Grant administration. Custer's virtuous decision to sacrifice himself and his troop to Crazy Horse's Indian horde to right the political wrongs provides one more example of the American respect for moral idealism. Thus Custer's military defeat is rewritten into an ethical victory for American culture, while the Indian was once again reduced to the immoral, physical foil of the superior white male. The essential concept supporting white cultural superiority to Natives was kept intact: even in a battle won by the Indians.

During this era of filmmaking, overtly racist depictions of Natives were routinely employed in the narrative. Within this construct Hollywood becomes a contributing factor to the oppression and exploitation of Natives. Convinced by film that Natives are savage and uncivilized, American audiences are content to allow government management of Indian affairs. The obvious suggestion of cultural and racial superiority of Anglo Americans over Indian peoples grants the public a dispensation for any transgressions assessed against Natives. Because in an age dominated by the belief in the Indian as the "Vanishing American," since the only law savages understand was force, and if some Indians were to survive in American society they must therefore be governed in the only way they understood: by the force of arms required to control childish creatures.

According to Fanon, Europe's racist language of authority becomes the lynchpin in governing Natives; making sure that the people of color know this is part of their proper management by White Culture. In his classic study of colonialism's psychological effect on the Black male, *Black Skin, White Masks* (1952), Frantz

Fanon condemns the paternalistic voice used by colonialist (Whites) to communicate with the colonized (Blacks and Arabs) as a tool used to reinforce the racial dominance of the White colonizer over the colored Native. As the colonizer, the White (in this case, French) society imposes their language upon the dominated colored Natives. This language becomes the voice of power that all members of society must speak in order to survive in the new racially hierarchical community. Unfortunately for the Native, the language is foreign to them and their ability to master the tongue is dependent on how much education in the colonizer's schools they are granted, or the level of interaction they have with the master race. Native attempts to speak the language of power are seen as humorous to the colonizer, and any opportunity to ridicule or demean the Native's speech reinforces the cultural and intellectual superiority of the colonizer.

The resulting pidgin interpretation of the foreign language by the colonized generates one factor by which the colonizer judges the intelligence of the Native. To exacerbate the condition colonists reduce themselves to the level of the colonized by speaking the pidgin language to Natives, so that the inferior Native may be better understood by the White master.[31] The cinematic voice of Indians will be very much affected by this mentality. In Cecil B. DeMille's *Unconquered* (1947), a fictitious account of the 1763 Pontiac War along the British-controlled Appalachian frontier, a scene has Captain Christopher Holden (Gary Cooper) enter the hostile Huron village under the leadership of Chief Guyasuta (Boris Karloff) to rescue the White woman Abigail (Abby) Martha Hale (Paulette Goddard). During the encounter Guyasuta responds to Holden's actions with one and two syllable grunt-like English words. Holden gains paternal control of the situation by answering back Guyasuta in loud, very deliberate one and two syllable English. Holden rescues the woman by

94

tricking the monosyllabic, superstitious Indian with the resourcefulness of European technology. Guyasuta's limited English thus identifies him as just another ingenuous and stupid Native.

Holden mesmerizes the simple-minded Guyasuta with the magnetic features of a compass. Holden and his female charge make their escape as Guyasuta's medicine man futilely seeks to remove the curse the British colonist has placed on the arrow-like object pointing at Guyasuta's heart who has frantically attached rifles and steel tomahawks to his belt in a desperate attempt to protect himself from this powerful White man's "magic.". Guyasuta is unaware that the metal in the rifles and tomahawks draw the compass needle towards themselves, and him. A viewer of this scene need only hear the dialogue between Holden and Guyasta to predict the results of this encounter. Because of the institutionalized American conception of Natives derived from the White (sub)Conscience, DeMille depicts the White/Native verbal exchange in the clearest of colonizer voices—a conversation dominated by the more technologically astute i.e. intelligent White colonizer.

According to Fanon, the colonialist rationale for speaking to Natives in this dialect invariably projects a condescending opinion of the latter. The reason they speak to Natives in pidgin, rather than the proper idiom, is because the White believes the Colored is too dim-witted to understand him/her if they spoke the correct tongue.[32] In addition to the patronizing use of language to reduce the colonized, the personified stereotypes of Natives enhance the covert racist agenda the White colonialist refuses to acknowledge. Thus, the verbal exchange between a white officer and an Indian chief in *Unconquered* manages to convey the colonialist use of language to sustain the inferior status of Indians, a national concept held by most Americans.

During the 1930s and '40s a plethora of westerns sustained equally offensive images of Indians. Whether it be the drunken Mohawks in *Drums Along the Mohawk* (1939), who sobered up enough to try sadistically to burn an American captive alive, or the dim-witted Indian attack on the train in DeMille's *Union Pacific* (1939), where a carefully planned ambush is turned into a carnage of absurdity and slaughter when the Indians are unable to understand such modern wares as a piano, a derby hat and a woman's corset.[33] American audiences are exposed to the Native behavior colonizer communities consider normal. These images help create the American construct of its world where racist, anti-Indian film depictions are an expression of reality. In this cultural environment biased Indian images have as significant a role to play as the metaphoric passenger list in *Stagecoach*, or the historic value of William Rogers taming of the frontier in the name of Progress.

Applying Goldberg's analysis of racist thinking to that of a colonizer mentality and the standardized use of Indian stereotyping in westerns, the negative depiction of Indians in cinema "is not simply a matter of overgeneralization grounded in conceptual mistakes and generating factual errors."[34] The Indian image has both cultural and social meaning, and in both cases the exploitative and oppressive nature of white/Native relations is justified by the innate superiority of one (whites), and the obvious inferiority of the other (Indians). Within the social milieu of a pre-World War II America, the national identity was still fueled by the racialized language of Social Darwinism and eugenics. Therefore the film images of Indians helped maintain a racialized discourse of Natives, thus sustaining a racist culture. It is a culture motivated by the capitalist-driven needs evolving out of colonialist exploitation.

The nature of the aforementioned ideology requires no concealment of racist agendas, no subliminal meanings; it is the communities understanding that the racialized social structure in place is a result of some pseudo-scientific rationale or the extension of a national myth. Race is the purveyor of the nation's raison d'être; its good fortune comes from the racial difference existing between themselves (white), and those they exploit (colored). From this position of power mainstream America and its media outlets remind themselves, and those within earshot, that the current social structure is a result of providence, science, technology, or a variation of any of the three. Guilt is absolved by the replacing of it with accusations. As Memmi explains, the colonizer "will persist in degrading them, using the darkest colors to depict them. If need be he will act to devalue them, annihilate them."[35]

During the pre-World War II era of American cinema Indian images justified national economic and political ascendancy and the two-tiered social relationship between whites and people of color. Native culture and reality had no place in this system. In westerns the narrative did not warrant the depiction of multi-dimensional Native characters, possessed with spirit, intelligence and humanity. The era did not call for it, but as social times changed after the victory over an inhumane racist, killing machine, post-World War II America had to distance itself from an ideology dangerously too close to the concepts held by its defeated foe, Nazi Germany. The fresh beginning called for new, less racist images of the other, and for Native Americans the change in social attitudes held great hope for new, and more complex, portrayals of Natives. However, the need to defend an ever improving standard of living, and the persistence of the White (sub)Conscience, generated a new image of Indians more insidious than the colonizer mentality driven savage used in pre-World War II cinema.

Post-World War II Hollywood envisioned a reconstructed Indian image that Americans were to sympathize with, and accept into their social bosom, but the resilient character of the White (sub)Conscience ensured that this alleged "new" portrayal would maintain the critical concepts supporting Anglo American superiority over Natives. No longer acceptable as the singularly evil creature of the pre-World War II cinema, American Indian imagery took on a new look, but the meaning remained the same. The new Indian depiction has a more noble and positive façade; however, a paternalistic depiction of Indians now creates a white/Indian relationship where whites benevolently introduce Indians into a complex and modern world. Still hampered by the vestiges of a "savage" education, Indians are unable to truly grasp the concepts of democracy, capitalism and the benefits associated with these concepts. It is the "great white father," and sometimes mother, that guide the Indian through this maze of progress.

Within this image the Indian is still characterized as child-like, savage, and ingenuous, but it is done in a manner meant to engender sympathy and deceptive respect for Indians. The only real change in this new Indian, a "good Indian," is the replacement of the overt racialized language of the colonizer mentality with a less offensive, yet highly effective, caricature still imbued with inferior images of "Indian" Americans have come to accept as "real." Americans merely experience the submergence of the racist ideology into the unconscious mind of the nation. Americans were no longer subjected to the racist depiction of evil, demonized Indians (although, for the sake of contrast, Hollywood would keep bad Indians in its scripts), the innovative "new" Indian image now masks the exploitative and oppressive relationship between whites and Natives behind a paternalistic image that protects the viewer from the racist language of an archaic age.

This image will dominate cinematic portrayal of Indians into the twenty-first century. Indian depictions still carry the old racialized message to the national subliminal mind, but now in a "benevolent and respectful" characterization, that acts as a statement to its viewers that sustain the racial and moral superiority of white Americans over Native Americans. Despite appearances to create a more inclusive image of Indians the ideological power of the White (sub)Conscience prevent Hollywood from depicting anything more than its own national iconographic idea of what is an Indian. The image remains the one formed over two hundred years of racist, colonizer influenced literature, research and popular culture. While it is the paternalist white in the "good Indian" films of the 1950s that generate the most recognizable image of Indians a generation of "baby boomers" will know as the "real" Indian, the 1930s and '40s Indian helped create the ambiguous distinction Americans will hold on Indians.

Television rerun Indians will create enough of a diversion in the childhood minds of its viewers that the youngsters will never understand how Indians can be so vile and destructive in one film, be so passive and dependent in another. Television stations ran the films they felt most entertained its audience; from a purely economic position, television programmers gave viewers what they (viewers) wanted to see. One late night they wanted to see a pathological savage threatening a wagon train or an isolated family of settlers. On Saturday they maybe felt like watching an American frontiersman or compassionate soldier save Indians from unscrupulous Whites who convince bad Indians to endanger hard-working White settlers.

Regardless of the mood the viewer was in, rest assured, the Indian image he/she watched held steadfast to the age-old characterizations that defended the foundation of America's exploitative society and its unending abuse of Native rights. The 1930s and '40s cinematic Indian transitioned the literary national mythology of "savage" and "sadistic" Indians opposing the westward movement of Progress onto the silver screen. The "new" cinematic Indian of the 1950s moves the depiction of Indians to the subliminal mind level of the White (sub)Conscience, a more deceptive and productive manner of defending White Supremacy. An ideology that eases the national conscience as Americans can revel in their compassionate treatment of Natives, all the while insensitive to the real plight of Natives struggling for self-determination and control of their own resources and future.

ENDNOTES CHAPTER 3

[1] Ray B. Brown, "Foreword," *Hollywood as Historian*, edited by Peter C. Rollins, Lexington: University of Kentucky Press, (1983), ix.

[2] Peter C. Rollins, "Introduction," *Hollywood as Historian*, 1.

[3] Peter Biskind, *Seeing is Believing: How Hollywood Taught us to stop Worrying and love the Fifties*, New York: Pantheon Books, (1983), 2-6.

[4] Not to be confused with authentic, Hollywood is adept at finding experts to reproduce Indian clothing, props and scenery. These are the alluring, flashy, shining features that grab the viewer's attention. This element is the hook: the story itself reels in the unsuspecting prey.

[5] Althea C. Huston, et al, *Big World, Small Screen: The Role of Television in American Society*, Lincoln: University of Nebraska Press, (1992), 21.

[6] Ibid.

[7] Huston, 22.

[8] John A. Price, "The Stereotyping of North American Indians in Motion Pictures," *Ethnohistory*, (1973), 20(2): 153-171.

[9] Albert Memmi, *The Colonizer and the Colonized*, London: Earthscan Publications, (1990) c1965, 86-87.

[10] See Edward W. Said, *Orientalism*, New York: Vintage Books, (1979) c1978.

[11] See Richard Drinnon, *Facing West: The Metaphysics of Indian-Hating and Empire-Building*, New York: Schocken Books, (1980).

[12] See Richard Slotkin, *Regeneration Through Violence: The Mythology of the American Frontier, 1600-1860*, Middletown, Connecticut: Wesleyan University Press, (1973); *The Fatal Environment: The Myth of the Frontier in the Age of Industrialization, 1800-1890*, Middletown, Connecticut: Wesleyan University Press, (1985); and *Gunfighter Nation: The Myth of the Frontier in Twentieth-Century America*, Norman: University of Oklahoma Press, (1992).

[13] See Amy Kaplan, *The Anarchy of Empire in the Making of U.S. Culture*, Cambridge: Harvard University Press, (2002).

[14] David Theo Goldberg, *Racial Subjects: Writing on Race in America*, New York: Routledge, (1997), 8.

[15] Drinnon, xxvii.

[16] Between 1932 and 1948 Johnny Weissmuller appeared in twelve *Tarzan* films that depicted Natives in the most vulgar and offensive images. The highly popular film series provide its audience with the many stereotypes of "deepest, darkest Africa's" inhabitants; lustful, bloodthirsty, sadistic, dim-witted can describe a *Tarzan* Native. Not surprisingly, these images have much in common with the way Hollywood portrayed Indians during this period.

[17] Slotkin, *Gunfighter Nation*, 304.

[18] Slotkin, *Gunfighter Nation*, 306.

[19] J.P. Telotte, "A Fate Worse Than Death: Racism, Transgression and Westerns," *Journal of Popular Film and Television*, (1998) Fall, 26:3, 120-127. Telotte's article examines the prevalent myth depicting Indian depravity towards white women, and the decision of a white man to kill a white woman, rather than leave her with "a fate worse than death." This "fate worse than death" mindset, fueled by the age-old American fear of miscegenation, defines a critical feature of the White (sub)Conscience. The use of the Indians as rapist theme deflects the ideology's concern for race mixing and the social consequences of this "depraved" behavior. "Fate worse than death" places the onus of racial intolerance on the lustful savage who wishes to defile the flower of American (White) womanhood, because it is the Indian who wishes to abuse and destroy that which is not his. The besieged Whites use force only to defend themselves. Killing a White woman is done only to prevent the real tragedy—allowing an Indian to have sexual intercourse with a White woman. To paraphrase Goldberg, "Race is irrelevant, but race is everything."

[20] In *Regeneration Through Violence* (1973), Richard Slotkin introduces the concept of the White frontiersman who goes to live amongst the Natives. He becomes such an expert at all Native traditions that he becomes the "Man who knows Indians." According to Slotkin, the "man who knows Indians" is an American "cultural" archetype functioning within the context of the "myth of the frontier." As Slotkin will argue in the remainder of his "Frontier Myth" trilogy, the "man who knows Indians" will be employed in U.S. popular culture and foreign policy as the authority on Native society.

[21] Frantz Fanon, *The Wretched of the Earth*, New York: Grove Press Inc., (1966) c1961, 34.

[22] Based on the incompetent martial skills demonstrated by Indians in Hollywood films one is hard pressed to use the term warrior in the same context of Indian.

[23] See "Mythical Portrait of the Colonized" in Albert Memmi's *The Colonizer and the Colonized*.

[24] Alice P. Sterner, "A Guide to the Discussion of the Technicolor Screen Version of *Northwest Passage*," *Photoplay Studies* 6, no. 9 (1940).

[25] Jacquelyn Kilpatrick, *Celluloid Indians: Native Americans in Film*, Lincoln: University of Nebraska Press, (1999), 50.

[26] Incidentally, the Dakota Territory in *They Died with Their Boots On* bears a strange resemblance to the Punjab region of northern India where Flynn had fought Sur Khan in *Light Brigade*, and Douglas Fairbanks, Jr. and Cary Grant had outwitted the Thugs in *Gunga Din*.

[27] Michael Hilger, *From Savages to Nobleman: Images of Native Americans in Film*, Lanham, Maryland: The Scarecrow Press, (1995), 69.

[28] Although the gesture may suggest the benevolent nature of white men, it can also be interpreted as a sign of disgust by the white for a defeated foe that did not merit a warrior's death. A popular myth developed in many Hollywood films about Indian men was their desire to die in combat as a real warrior, rather as a decrepit old man lying on his back. Thus, if Hollywood argues, for an Indian, death in combat is the only way to die as a man, if the white foe refuses to kill the defeated Indian doesn't this suggest Hollywood's own manipulation of film myth to demean and belittle Indians as part of their own biased, even racist, conceptualization of Natives?

[29] Crazy Horse is rescued by one of the dozens of Indians who are roaming the fort grounds buying whiskey and rifles from unscrupulous federal Indian agents. Perhaps like the Latin American, or Middle Eastern, immigrants of today, the Indian presence within a white man's sanctuary is a violation of the latter's innate right to security. Only after Custer denied the Indians access to the fort was the place safe for the white inhabitants.

[30] This symbolic gesture also expresses the military cooperation existing between the two allies in their struggle against the Nazis.

[31] Fanon, *Black Skin, White Masks*, New York: Grove Press, (1967) c1952, 30-31.

[32] Fanon, *Black Skin, White Masks*, 31-32.

[33] As soon as the attack on the train begins the "real" image of Indians is portrayed to the audience. It is the modern gadgets found on the train that help combine two features of Indian-ness most fundamental to the White Conscience and its colonizer mentality subdivision—brutish savage and childish buffoon. Modern technology proves too intellectually complex for the Indians to ignore. Along with the murdering of the passengers on the train the Indians will assault a piano; another will unreel bolts of cloth and attach them to his horse's tail; one impales a derby on his rifle; another tries to figure out a women's corset, and eventually decides it is meant to go around a horse's neck; and the final act of ironic absurdity has a group of Indians being frightened by a wooden cigar store Indian.

[34] David Theo Goldberg, *Racist Culture: Philosophy and the Politics of Meaning*, Malden, Massachusetts: Blackwell Publishers, (1993), 128.

[35] Memmi, 120.

Chapter 4
The "Good Indian" Film:
Dependent Indians
And
Great Fathers.[1]

After World War II Americans understood the need to confront the social paradox that just witnessed the United States battle against the tyrannical agenda of fascist states while the nation upheld its own racist attitude towards people of color. Colonialism's age was coming to an end. Great Britain slowly divested itself of its empire holdings, as did many of its neighbors. In those cases where European powers refused to recognize the shifting winds of freedom, colonial subjects launched wars of liberation to remedy the situation. Although the United States would itself deny any colonizer behavior in its past, it is evident in the cinematic use of Indians that Hollywood reflected the nation's awareness of global social inequalities.

Over the course of the fifteen years following the end of World War II Hollywood, keen to changing social moods, developed new Indian representations in their works. The post-World War II western genre, more specifically 1950s films, introduced America to an Indian representation that highlighted the nation's perceived progressive social conscience. The industry softened the Indian image of previous generations to include what Hollywood considered more compassionate depictions. Although the murderous savage managed to survive the scriptwriter's editing, liberal-minded Hollywood also produced an Indian Americans could sympathize with. It was the era of the "good Indian" western.

Hollywood helped Americans see Indians adopting positive characteristics more representative of middle-American values, and thus exhorted the virtues of the nation's alleged progressive social conscience currently in progress. These Indians battled the same injustices that Anglo- American heroes had previously done. As far as Hollywood was concerned, it was time for them to depict the nation's acceptance of its Indian brethren into the social circle of middle-America. Although the actual civil rights struggle began a few years after Delmer Daves' *Broken Arrow* (1950), Hollywood was introducing its audience to images of people of color that, in essence, prepared society for the imminent social struggle already brewing in federal courts. If the civil rights movement was to succeed, Americans had to accept people of color as socially acceptable beings. Hollywood acted as a visual and commercial conduit for the growing recognition by Americans to changing social attitudes on race. Thus, from an altruistic perspective, one could argue Hollywood foretold, or, at the very least, helped groom the nation for, the coming of the civil rights movement. Nothing could be further from the truth.

In its own ingenuous and naïve manner, Hollywood was merely mimicking generations of American literary and cinematic architects who had employed Indian images to assert contemporary political or social ideologies. There was nothing philanthropic in the manner in which Hollywood portrayed its "good Indian." Since early nationhood during the 1790s Americans have waged the conflicting battle between capitalist growth and Native sovereignty. During the next century and a half a diverse set of reformers (government officials, concerned citizens, and missionaries) designed Indian policy rooted in inaccurate and fallacious beliefs about Native behavior. It is an identity suggesting the much-needed intervention of the master White race to assist the Native people. Yet, somehow despite these philanthropic actions Natives will still lose much of their lands, experience grave population decreases, and expose themselves to cultural genocide. Unprepared to see the Natives outside of their colonizer mentality, Americans manage only to make the suffering of Natives more tolerable to the national conscience.

Assisting Natives was designed without consideration for the consequences of these actions on Natives, suffice to say, these choices did met the satisfaction of the Americans affecting Indian policy. Ever since the United States first gained a limited military advantage over Native Americans after the Battle of Fallen Timbers in 1794,[2] the "Indian Question" has perplexed the most progressive politician. Although defenders of Indian rights are genuinely concerned for Native welfare, the White (sub)Conscience ideology fueling the extermination and exploitation of millions of people of color, in the name of capitalism, identifies the lazy, technologically inept Native that anti-colonialist scholar Albert Memmi describes as the key component to the White defense of colonialism.[3] Thus American (White) support of Indian rights manifests itself from this reference point, and every defender of Indians preserves the same insensitive opinions, fostered from the hateful dialectic of colonialist conquest, for the very people they claim to represent. From the country's inception its Indian reformers will engage in this cultural conflict of interest and decide the future of people they have, and more importantly show, little interest in really knowing.

As mentioned in Chapter 2, even the most illustrious of early American Indian benefactors, Thomas Jefferson, held a less than auspicious track record of recognizing Native rights. The seeds of the White (sub)Conscience were already taking root in the Jeffersonian period. As described in Bernard Sheehan's *Seeds of Extinction* (1973), the essence of Jeffersonian Indian policy was promulgated in White intellectual discourse seeking the salvation of the "Noble Savage" the fledgling state was now saddled with. Undermining the desire to save the Native was an insidious racist imagery of the Indian that precluded any equitable relationship between government and Native societies. Despite the superficial claim of their desire to help the Indian, Jeffersonian humanitarians harbored biased perceptions of Natives that instinctively placed the latter on a lower social, or moral, scale.

The Ojibwe historian Rebecca Kugel illustrates a classic example of late-Jeffersonian era intolerance of Native culture in the behavior of Protestant missionary, William Boutwell. Arriving amongst Ojibwe living on the western shores of Lake Superior, along the present-day Minnesota/Wisconsin border, in the spring of 1832 as a member of United States Indian Agent Henry Schoolcraft's expedition seeking the source of the Mississippi River, Boutwell described in journals and letters his abhorrence for the honor dance ceremony the Ojibwe performed as a symbolic gesture of the alliance between the two people.[4]

The Ojibwe envisioned Boutwell's visit as an ambassadorial gesture between two sovereign people negotiating to reach a bilateral accordance. Like so many other reform-oriented Americans Boutwell failed to acknowledge his Ojibwe hosts as legitimate social equals. In fact, Kugel describes the subtle, yet critical, change in language used by the federal government to distinguish United States/Indian relations. In the wording of the treaty of 1825, Kugel claims, "The Americans departed from the egalitarian kin term of 'brother' and began to address the Ojibwe as 'children,' a highly charged term that implied subordination and dependence."[5] At the very moment that the United States was negotiating from a reciprocal position it was already embracing the dominant status towards the Native Americans; a view engendered in the white supremacist ideology applied to the colonized people of color, and a concept quite evident in the assimilationist policies of the late-nineteenth century I will address later.

During the middle-half of the nineteenth century Native Americans were subjected to an all out assault on their mortal existence. Ignoring the apparent success of assimilationist policy occurring amongst the Five Civilized Tribes, Jeffersonian reformers sought for all Indians, rather than respect the Native's commitment to Americanization, Andrew Jackson era politicians applied the more expedient, and profitable, policy of Indian removal. By whatever means deemed necessary; political manipulation, bribery, coercion, cajoling, or military force, by the beginning of the Civil War most Native Americans living east of the Mississippi River lost their indigenous lands to White settlers; being removed to Indian Territory. After the Civil War, President Ulysses S. Grant's so called Peace Policy, a "carrot and stick" strategy,[6] generated to bring peace to the Great Plains for further White expansion west, failed to bring Natives justice, economic prosperity or peace.[7] However, government increased spending on Indian education during the 1870s motivated a new generation of Indian reformers to step-up the "assimilationist crusade,"[8]

Helen Hunt Jackson's exposé of America's dismal Indian policy record, *A Century of Dishonor* (1881), shifted the American public's attention from the genocidal and costly Indian wars on the Great Plains to adopting instead the notion of saving the Natives. It was during this period of social consciousness that reformers once again revitalized the American desire to civilize the "savage Indian." All-White organizations such as the Indian Rights Association and the Lake Mohonk Friends of the Indians Conference took it upon themselves to lift the Native from darkness into the civilized light of American society. Lakota historian, Vine Deloria, Jr. keenly points out that Darwinian theory shaped the Indian reformists' reasoning. Considering the American Anglo-Saxon race as the summit of social realization, embodied in their mastery of modern technology, it was only logical that colored races represented the lower strata of the human race. The responsibility to "raise the barbarous people" fell upon the superior American Aryan race. Indian reformers believed the Natives to be "far down the evolutionary ladder, but capable of climbing toward enlightenment if provided with the opportunity."[9]

Based on the aforementioned racial premise, late-nineteenth century Indian policy centered on assimilation and the Native's ability to adapt to American society. The two-pronged centerpiece of this strategy was education and land severalty; each goal defined the American concept of what Indians should be, never do the reformers consider the attitude of Natives to develop this strategy.

Small wonder Natives will experience little benefits from programs meant to improve their social place. As mentioned above, the concept of Indian education lacked a Native agenda; in fact, the premise behind Indian education was based strictly on the idea of lifting the Native from his/her savage state, up to the more advanced White civilization. Convinced that exposure to Indian culture at home hindered this process reformers recommended removal from homes as the best strategy for educating the Indian children. Young students were sent away to Indian boarding schools in far off places such as Sherman Indian School in Riverside, California and the United States Industrial School at Carlisle, Pennsylvania. The primary function of these schools was to teach Indians a technical vocation while inculcating them with a strong dose of American values: Anglo-Saxon, Protestant values.

The decision to remove Indian children from family homes was popular because it was the most obvious choice to keep them away from the harmful influence of their parent's primitive Indian ways; the practice was not always beneficial to the Native children. In the winter of 1886-1887, one-hundred and sixty

Chiricahua Apache children were removed from their families and sent Carlisle: twenty-nine died of tuberculosis.[10] The death of these Native children brought little sympathy from the director of the school.

A specialist in Native American health, H. Henrietta Stockel skillfully points out that in a letter to the Commissioner of Indian affairs, dated May 24, 1889, the superintendent of the Carlisle Indian School, Captain R. H. Pratt brought attention to the alarmingly high mortality rate amongst the Chiricahua children: however, Pratt placed blame for the deaths on the victims themselves. Pratt claimed the deaths were caused by "conditions outside of his control."[11] Stockel's most scathing indictment of Pratt was "his statement about 'sifting' the Chiricahuas and 'the unhealthy ones disposed of' is chilling, reminiscent of the attitudes of those responsible for the Holocaust in Europe not so long ago."[12]

The letter to the Commissioner originated from the mind of the person entrusted with the education of the Native children. Tinged by a eugenicist philosophy, and a barbarous subject, Pratt's comments are representative, not only of his contemporary Indian reformers, but of colonizer mentality Americans, who believe that the ills that plagued Native Americans were brought upon themselves because of their failure to adapt to the superior American society. While Pratt focused on "saving the child," other Indian reformers concentrated on the age-old American icon: the yeoman farmer.

Key Indian reformers of the time staunchly agreed that it was imperative to remove Indians from their traditional existence and provide them the necessary tools to make the successful transition to American society. Massachusetts' senator Henry Dawes, the leading voice in land severalty for Natives argued that the government "should draw [the Indian] through their affections, their instincts, and their tastes up to our civilization, and get them to dissolve their relations with the tribe."[13]

Turning the Natives into yeoman farmers was the first step in modernity's battle to destroy the vulgar primitive behavior of Indians. The General Allotment Act of 1887 (Dawes Act) was the mechanism the federal government used to move the Indian toward assimilation. The Dawes Act allotted the Natives 160 acres of land that were to be used for cultivation; that on many reservations the assigned lands proved arable-poor was irrelevant. It may not be the legal step many historians claim removed millions of Native lands from indigenous Americans, but as historian Frederick Hoxie attentively posits, the Dawes Act was a "statement of intent." Hoxie further claims:

> At its core, the law was an assertion that the gap between the two races would be overcome and that Indians would be incorporated into American society. They would farm, participate in government, and adopt "higher" standards of behavior. The statute assumed that land ownership, citizenship, and education would alter traditional cultures, bringing them to "civilization.[14]

The Dawes Act was representative of the consensus opinion of White America's plan to save the Indian. Destroying all vestiges of traditional life and forcing the Indian to assimilate to, what for them (Natives) was, a foreign culture provided reformist the recipe for destroying Native American societies. By the end of the 1910s even the most ardent Indian reformist appeared to have given up on their charges, wracked by economic, political, psychological misery, Native Americans found themselves culturally living up to the national myth of the "Vanishing American." The 1928 Merriam Report reintroduced the Native problem to federal officials and the public: soon a new wave of reformers began a crusade to save "their Indians."

The Merriam Report had a sobering effect on Congress. The report strongly suggested a failed federal Indian policy. Indian reformers lauded the disturbing results justifying their beliefs regarding the inhumane assimilationist and allotment policies practiced against Natives. Yet even the pro-Indian reformist of the 1920s and 1930s, who fought hard to defend Natives, failed to recognize the sovereign rights as nations of Natives having distinct cultural properties. Commissioner of Indian Affairs John Collier helped pass the Wheeler-Howard Indian Rights Act (1934); also known as the Indian Reorganization Act (IRA), or Indian New Deal, to protect Indian rights. Yet, as historian Brian Dippie has noted, during the 1920s Native Americans became political symbols contrasting the excesses of capitalist exploitation of natural resources, rather than as individuals, or nations, seeking only the rudimentary essentials to experience the dignified life both American encroachers and Indian reformers were denying them.

Reaching back into the Indian stereotypes of an earlier generation, the "Noble Savage" returned once again, this time as the consummate conservationist, which in turn, implied that the Indian his/herself must be conserved.[15] The Natives became mere relics to be preserved. Early twentieth century anthropologists, such as Franz Boas, had already created what Dippie describes as, "Salvage Ethnography,"[16] the accumulation and preservation of Native artifacts to record the presence of the "Vanishing American" before his/her anticipated demise. According to Dippie, Indian Reorganization proponents took the ethnographic principle of preservation to the paramount level by "freezing the Indian situation where it was."[17]

Despite his concerns for protecting Native Americans, John Collier maintained a narrow interpretation of Indian rights and cultural identity.

115

During the 1920s Collier was introduced to, and subsequently mesmerized by, the New Mexico Pueblo culture; they in turn, became his Native litmus test group. In an ironic reversal of the old assimilationist position of Jeffersonians and late-nineteenth century reformers, Collier insisted that all Indians develop"...a closely knit communal existence similar to the New Mexico Pueblos...."[18]

Collier's IRA succeeded in destroying traditional Native governance on those reservations accepting the Indian New Deal, and imposing a distinctively American political institution upon the Natives. In his economic study of the effects of the Indian New Deal on the South Dakota Lakota reservations, Thomas Biolsi describes the consequences of New Deal relief and relief work as reinforcing "the artificial nature of the reservation economies and, thus, the dependence of the Lakota upon the OIA (Office of Indian Affairs)."[19] The effect of IRA policy was to further strengthen Indian dependency upon the federal government and to establish dictatorial regimes, such as Dick Wilson's mid-1970s Pine Ridge autocracy, which, exploited the Lakota residents as a surrogate for Corporate America energy agencies, with the compliance of the federal agencies vested with responsibility to protect their charges.

Thus, as well meaning 1950s Hollywood film makers generated their new Indian, they were doing nothing more than re-inventing America's most glaring reminder of its colonizer past: the Native. Over the course of the previous two centuries the Indian provided America its collective panacea to sooth its colonizer (White) conscience by supposedly proving their own savagery and hence a need to be dominated. Little wonder the Hollywood Indian of the 1950s contained many of the enigmatic images of "Indians" that Anglo society had come to accept as normal and accurate. In its desire to present a more sympathetic Indian more

116

fitting of the changing social climate, Hollywood was merely reshuffling its souvenir deck of Indian playing cards. The game remained the same. Using the same pictures of Indians, paternalistic directors and writers claimed to depict new, more realistic Indians as a way to honor them, yet national stereotypes of Indians continued to dominate plots.

Three key plot elements develop the subliminal message to the viewers of the new western films; the noble savage, the paternalistic White male figure, and the "Bad" Indian. Each of the "Childhood Indian" films used as examples in this work adhere to the radical "new" images of Indians that will dominate Hollywood westerns to the end of the century. Presented in different forms and with different storylines, the fundamental Indian story held true to national myths, and notwithstanding its alleged purpose generated images no more innovative than what first generation of European colonists held of Natives. The "New Indian" outline produced the essential characteristics Americans held of Indians, thus reiterating the national myth of Indian dependency through one more media apparatus.

Although Hollywood claimed to honor Native Americans in the new westerns, it did little more than sustain age-old paternalistic images of Indians that did nothing more than obfuscate the nation's terrible treatment of Natives. The first of the so called "good Indian" films that will surreptitiously defend the fundamental principles of America's colonizer ideology was Delmer Daves' *Broken Arrow* (1950), despite its pretentious self-indulging claims to honoring its Indian subjects.

No "good Indian" film can exist without its most critical character, the noble savage. Americans had already come to know the early nineteenth century works of James Fenimore Cooper's Chingachcook in the immensely popular Hawkeye novels, Washington Irving's short story *Philip of Pokanoket*, or John

Augustus Stone's play *Metamora; or the Last of the Wampanoags*.[20] Thus, one is hard-pressed to call Hollywood's "new" Indian innovative, yet the industry will pride itself in this characterization.

When Daves introduced his Metamora-like figure of Cochise (Jeff Chandler) to film audiences in *Broken Arrow* he was praised for his "pioneering" depiction of a noble, cultured Indian. As the Friar's observed, "Audiences were grabbed by their throats and large, liberal doses of a new patent medicine were rammed down their gullets.... These films were to be the cathartic to cleanse us all. Indians would be proud, noble, decent, but oppressed people."[21] Chandler's handsome, athletic-looking Cochise appeared every bit the gentleman and diplomat. Yet even as Americans were introduced to this innovative Indian, Daves was unable to escape his ideological legacy. Regardless of how noble the nation's savages may appear, they can never appreciate the full virtues of American culture (i.e. democracy and self-autonomy) without the assistance of their Great White Father.[22] This second significant factor in the screenplay, perhaps the most critical, helps to suggest the truly backward nature of even the most competent of the Native leaders. Without this plot development the director is unable to sustain the generally appreciated and accepted superiority of American society.

Therefore, it is the White Tom Jeffords (James Stewart) who initiates peace talks between the Americans and Cochise's Chiricahua Apaches. Motivated by economic principles (to protect his government contracted mail carriers) Jeffords exemplifies the most altruistic behaviors of the American citizen. Jeffords first obtains the services of a friendly Apache (a cinematic oxymoron at the time) to learn the Apache's language.[23] After he has mastered not only the language, but Chiricahua culture itself, Jeffords embarks alone on the dangerous journey into

118

the homelands of the Chiricahua with the apocalyptic advise from his Apache teacher that no White man had seen Cochise in person and lived since the Apache began his war against the Americans, yet the brave White peacemaker is undeterred.

Daves' script emphasizes the friendship developed between these two White and Red brothers. The premise of the story suggests the two men develop a friendship because of both of their strong desire to help their people, and the similarities in moral principles. Yet it is the White Jeffords who must face the most dangerous of challenges, including an attempted lynching by less racially sensitive Whites. Cochise stoically accepts the advice of Jeffords for peace negotiations and is impressed when Jeffords explains to him a superficial understanding of an Apache ceremonial dance. Every bit the "Man Who Knows Indians"[24] Jeffords displays a more superior base of learning than his Red "brother."[25]

While it is true the audience can sympathize with the more civilized Indian chief in *Broken Arrow*, the man is none the less a caricature figure of certain Indian-ness qualities (such as stoic, unemotional, and uncivilized) that provides the viewer the visual contrast between savage Indian and morally superior Whites. Cochise allows the audience to empathize with the plight of the "vanishing American," while reminding them that they have done everything in their power to prevent the Native's demise. If there was blame to be placed on the Indians downfall, it fell on the third important narrative factor to explain: the bad Indian.

To draw from a well known scientific axiom, "For every action, there is a reaction." Unable to admit complete Anglo American blame from atrocities committed against Natives, the White (sub)Conscience influences Hollywood's need to contrast Indian goodness with Indian malevolence. Thus, as Hollywood acts on its good intentions and portrays sympathetic

Indians, it comes without question that they must therefore counter a "good Indian" with the "bad Indian." This "bad Indian" is the reminder to the audience that regardless of how much civilization they are exposed to, no matter how many good Americans they come in contact with, Indians are only one misunderstanding away from returning to their savage origins. In the case of *Broken Arrow*, Geronimo (Jay Silverheels) played Cochise's foil, and challenged his chief's peace proposal with the Americans.[26] Geronimo and his renegade Apaches continued their war against the Whites, causing Cochise to rescue a stagecoach full of Americans Geronimo's warriors had attacked.

The film reaches a peaceful conclusion only after Jeffords' Indian maiden wife Sonseeahray (Debra Padget) is killed by bigoted whites and Cochise reminds Jeffords that his dead wife would not be pleased if he shed blood to avenge her death: therefore the two men must work harder to preserve the peace.[27] In the modern depiction of "bad Indians" it was only right that there be "bad Whites" once again to remind the audience that benevolent White behavior will overcome both "bad Indians" and "bad Whites." In the end, Jeffords' sacrifices help forge what the audience believes is a fair peace. Because aren't most Americans really like Jeffords? Americans did everything in their power to protect the Indians, if anything went wrong it was the fault of the "bad Indians," or at worst "bad Whites," who were an anomaly in their anti-Indian feelings.

Thus the "good Indian" film *Broken Arrow* acted as a cinematic metaphor of the altruistic spirit of the American people. Deep down Americans are good people; despite a few social miscreants, righteous behavior does win out in the end. As for the Indians, their social role is also clarified. The noble Cochise learned to appreciate peace only after the paternalistic White Jeffords taught him the value of racial/social harmony. A new generation of American film audiences was taught, in a more subtle narrative, the continued need for Americans to maintain social constraints over the still savage and unstable Native community.

Broken Arrow was Hollywood's first significant attempt to depict what it believed was a "new" Indian. Instead, it upheld a long tradition of Americans excusing injustices against Native Americans as manifested in the White (sub)Conscience. An example of the film's influence on contemporary westerns is a set of those infamous "childhood Indian" films I watched on Saturday afternoons including *Taza: Son of Cochise* (1954), *Sitting Bull* (1954), *Walk the Proud Land* (1956) and *Pillars of the Sky* (1956). Despite the innocuous lives of these films one must not brush side the significant influence they have on impressionable television viewers. Each of these "Childhood Indian" films succeeded in ascertaining long held paternalistic (colonizer) beliefs that Indian survival in the new social order is directly related to their acquiescence to American subjugation and benevolence.

Taza: Son of Cochise is the last installment of the "Jeff Chandler/Cochise" trilogy. Three years after the alleged end of the "Apache wars," on his deathbed Cochise asks his son Taza (Rock Hudson) to maintain the peace between his people and the Whites; to which Taza agrees. In Hollywood's version of Cochise's successor, Taza must battle his evil brother Naiche (Bart Roberts), who refuses to adopt the "ways of the White man." On the surface this story develops a rather benign suggestion of the age-old belief that Natives must assimilate in order to survive. However, the struggle between the two siblings contains far more insidious inferences. The brother's rivalry provides the perfect backdrop for the "good Indian" versus "bad Indian" archetype, which maintains the nation's schizophrenic adoration and abhorrence of Natives.

Taza can play the role of an American hero, but as an Indian, a menacing foil must be present to provide

121

the audience the recognizable contrast to the film's "good Indian;" an essential element in reminding viewers of the savage nature of Indians. Albert Memmi's "colonizer mythology" helps explains Hollywood's need to maintain long-standing myths in spite of the alleged progress of racial tolerance. Memmi explains the use of fictitious images of Natives as occupying "a choice place in colonialist ideology; a characterization which is neither true to life, or in itself incoherent, but necessary and inseparable within the ideology."[28] In the case of *Taza*, viewers were required to remember that despite their noble appearance an Indian is still an Indian. Regardless of their pathetic attempts to assimilate Natives posed a natural threat to civilized man (Americans), and only the intervention of Whites can prevent ascending into social chaos.

To further underscore this point in *Taza*, with the guidance of the army officer at the reservation Captain Burnett (Gregg Palmer), the script has Taza creating a provisional Apache police force, with makeshift cavalry uniforms and all: Gunga Din in moccasins. The benevolent Captain Burnett patiently nurtures Taza's frustrated attempts to gain control of his village while Naiche and Geronimo plot. In the end Taza proves his worthiness when he rescues Captain Burnett and his troop from a Naiche and Geronimo ambush, killing his brother in a hand-to-hand fight to determine the fate of his people.

Along the same logic of Memmi's "colonizer myth" that influences the "Good Indian/Bad Indian" character dichotomy, Hollywood doesn't mind the historical errors made in telling this [superficial] struggle between good and evil. It is true Cochise did have two sons at the time of his death in 1874, but further than that Hollywood goes beyond stretching the truth. Taza (Tahzay) did succeeded his father upon Cochise's death, but died of tuberculosis in 1876 while visiting Washington D.C. during the Centennial Celebration.

His much younger brother Naiche, perhaps sixteen at the time of his father's death, and who was later a victim of the Great Influenza Pandemic of 1919, never challenged his brother's succession. Naiche has become a revered figure in the Apache community for his nationalist struggle against American domination during the 1880s, and his portrait hangs next to that of his father's inside the Saint Joseph's Mission on the Mescalero Apache Reservation in New Mexico. Regardless of the truth, Hollywood's *Taza* proves a much more agreeable characterization of the idea that the American way was best for the Apaches, and thus by conforming to White wishes Taza fit the "Good Indian" image perfectly.

Along the "Gunga Din in Moccasins" trope, *Walk the Proud Land* (1956) exposes its viewers to those *Taza* Indian police officers, only this time without its famous chief. In the case of *Walk the Proud Land*, the "true" story of Indian Agent John Clum, the Indian police are the brainchild of the eastern-raised (i.e. Liberal), but firm, Clum (Audie Murphy). Based upon Woodworth Clum's 1936 biography of his father, *Walk the Proud Land* displays the fair-minded, law-abiding American social machine of the 1950s that was ready to bring justice and peace to the Third World. *Walk the Proud Land* gave its makers the mechanism to depict the far-sighted depth of American paternalism as its paves the way for the post-World War II world.

Arriving at the San Carlos Apache Reservation in the mid-1870s Clum believed that the best way to control the savage Apaches was to give them their own sense of self-determination. According to *Walk the Proud Land*, by creating an all-Indian police force and judiciary, Clum gave the Apaches the incentive to make peace with Whites and live happily ever after on their largely un-arable, alkaline riddled reservation soil. This film was produced a few years after the removal of John Collier as Commissioner of Indian Affairs, and the film bears a strange resemblance to the reservation governments resulting from the aforementioned 1934 Wheeler-Howard Indian Rights Act.   Clum demonstrated the unique qualities the modern-day American philanthropist, such as Edward Lansdale and his modernization of the government of South Vietnam.[29]

Guiding its audience through the most fundamental examples of the benevolent White master and his Native apprentice, *Walk The Proud Land* maintains the essential principles of the White (sub)Conscience while embracing the construct of the "good Indian" image. The film is an empathetic portrayal of the Apache warrior Taglito (Tommy Rall), who clumsily struggles to understand the "White Man's law." Under the patient direction of Clum, the Apache warrior learns the nuances of civilization, almost second nature to the Indian agent, and helped his White mentor fight off corrupt White businessmen from nearby Tucson (some two hundred miles from San Carlos in the real world) and incorrigible Indians (Jay Silverheels reprising his role as the omnipresent Indian bad guy, Geronimo), and bringing civil order to the Wild West.

By introducing American justice to the Indians, Hollywood's Clum carried the nation's "burden" to the uncivilized Natives, once again demonstrating the virtuous and benevolent nature of the White culture. In fighting White corruption, the modern-day liberal character shows he is willing to alienate his own kind for justice to the less fortunate of this world: in this case, Natives. The modern-day "White Man's Burden" complex creates a social dialogue nurturing the predisposed desired outcome. In *Racist Culture* (1993) David Theo Goldberg suggests modern-day cultures have rationalized the inferiority of Natives within a socio-political discourse.[30] Defenders of neo-colonizer behavior must thus intellectualize the dominant culture's paternalistic control of Natives, as being a byproduct of the latter's social inadequacy. As the audience witnesses the development of the socially inept Taglito into a semi-autonomous purveyor of American justice, Clum's character maintains the cultural racialized iconography of Indian/White relations essential to the veiled assertion of White cultural dominance.

Released two years before *Walk the Proud Land*, *Sitting Bull* (1954) held steadfast to the Delmer Daves' formula of the great Indian chief bringing peace between Indians and Whites. My fondest childhood memory of *Sitting Bull* was the stirring Indian refrain, "Great Spirit, as you led our fathers in the years of yore, lead us to the Happy Hunting Ground to dwell forever more."[31] Combined with the stoic presence of the great Sioux chief Sitting Bull (J. Carol Naish) this film left an indelible memory on one eight year old. Like the "Indian" song that affected me so strongly, much of *Sitting Bull*'s Indian-ness was founded on Hollywood filmmakers' use of the national pseudo-Indian iconography.

Never in the artistic class of *Broken Arrow*, *Sitting Bull* found large audiences on Saturday afternoon and late-night television programming, thus proving more successful a vessel of the White (sub)Conscience in reruns than during its original release. Like *Broken Arrow*, *Sitting Bull* used the context of a modernistic depiction of an Indian hero to reiterate the national mythology. Although the wise and articulate Sitting Bull is, according to the film title, the central character, it is the American officer Major Bob Parrish (Dale Robertson), who risks his career and life to bring peace between Indians and Whites, who embodies the individual qualities that will make him the appropriate hero of this film.

While Sitting Bull makes flowery speeches and alludes to the dying Indian culture, it is Parrish who is the man of action. It is Parrish who takes the risks that will lead to peace between the two people. He will have his rank reduced to captain because he disobeyed the orders of an Indian agent who was abusive to Indians; he lost his girlfriend because she became tired of his propensity to get in trouble for protecting the Indians; he even fights Crazy Horse (Iron Eyes Cody) in a man-to-man knife duel.[32] Later during the climactic "Battle of the Little Big Horn" Parrish and his Black sidekick, Sam,[33] hide from chasing Sioux behind tall sagebrush, only moments after the warriors had been within arms distance of the soldier and his guide.

To further demonstrate the superior principles of this man, after surviving the massacre, Parrish seeks out the victorious enemy, who incidentally are celebrating their victory oblivious to a large unit of U.S. forces heading straight to their encampment, to rescue them. Not because he hates Whites, or no longer respects his country, he does it because he is a humanitarian who wants to prevent any more bloodshed. These are the images that remind an American viewing audience how morally just the consummate White philanthropist is when put to the test. Australian cultural anthropologist Nicholas Thomas suggests that within a colonizer context this form of Native/White representation is a normal function of social legitimization. Although structured on a theoretical discourse of colonialism, Thomas' argument will hold true for the understanding of a film where a White man interacts with Natives. Thus, "where a discursive object, and its possible values and uses in a description or story are secure…one might say that a discourse is effectively policed;" Thomas adds, "it is organized in terms of a tacit interrogation that is unitary and dominant."[34]

Despite the name in the title of a Native leader, *Sitting Bull*'s script must conform to the collective needs of a society deeply absorbed in its colonizer past. A movie about an Indian chief necessitates characters the dominant culture can relate to, and identify as "one of their one." To further drive this point into the audience's social conscience the script will depict as many of the cultural myths of American superiority as can be applied in the flow of the story. When Sitting Bull rides into rescue Parrish from the firing squad that is to execute the officer for treason, the Indian chief chastises President Ulysses S. Grant for almost killing a true "patriotic son" of his people. When Sitting Bull rides off into the hills with the soundtrack refrain asking the Great Spirit to "lead us to the Happy Hunting Ground" the viewer understands that the days of a free Sitting Bull and his Sioux are numbered, and American benefactors such as President Grant and Bob Parrish will continue to do what they can to help the doomed Indian.

Where *Sitting Bull* helped reinforce the secular American frontier myth *Pillars of the Sky* validated the nation's continuous Christian struggle to subdue the godless heathen. Filmed in the breathtaking Oregon mountain wilderness, the movie distorts the 1855 Yakima War, and the image of one of the Native participants, the Yakamas' leader Kamiakin, to depict the ageless battle between the righteous Christian and Satan's minions. In a stroke of divine propaganda genius, director George Marshall uses Indians to tell the proverbial story of good versus evil. Marshall's first critical decision is the use of names to distinguish "good versus evil." The good Indians are identified by their Christian names, while the bad Indians are recognized by their Indian names. In this manner the viewer is able to tell a good Indian from a bad Indian, which is important because as Memmi argues, in the context of the colonizer's practice of generalizing about Natives, Whites are incapable of distinguishing between the Natives.[35]

The story of *Pillars of the Sky* begins with a misunderstanding between the Christianized Indians and government officials. When soldiers build a bridge to enter into the Indian reservation, a violation of the treaty between the two sides, the Christian Indians are convinced by the heathen Kamiakin to go on the warpath. Almost immediately the viewer is reminded that the partially converted Indian is still an Indian, and needs little pressure to revert to his savage origins, and rekindle irrational hatred for the White defenders of the Christianity.

The key figure in the dichotomous Indian relationship is the American missionary, Dr. Joseph Holden. Holden represents the strong-willed, benevolent Christian, devoid of any racially motivated hatred towards his flock. All the missionary wants to do is share his god with his Indian children. Be clear of one important factor; this son of Christ is no weakling. Holden, played by the physically imposing Ward Bond, is an individual blessed with a firm, forceful voice. He is the pious Christian soldier entering into battle with the Bible in one hand and a sword in the other. As a testament to his faith, Holden is willing to die for his belief. In his death Holden will ensure a Christian future for these Indians.

The film builds towards its climactic ending when an Indian boy attending Holden's missionary school repudiates his father, who has joined Kamiakin's hostiles, and his Indian way of life. The rift between father and son reassures the viewer that if given an opportunity to choose between a Christian (American) way of life and that of a godless Indian, once exposed to the virtues of the dominant Christian culture, an Indian child will forsake his past in order to live an honest, virtuous existence. In his aptly title tome *Slaves of the White Myth* Thomas Gladwin, assisted by Ahmad Saidin, presents a study of the psychological effects of neocolonialism. The authors suggest that the colonized elite seek to find acceptability from their White master's by mimicking both their behavior and customs. Gladwin writes, "Those locals who can afford to, quickly follow these same guidelines and go to the same places to be seen in white company, further setting themselves apart from their own 'inferior' people."[36] The boy's behavior works to remind the viewer of this colonizer axiom: the educated Native merely mimics his White master's actions, and remains the latter's inferior.

Emboldened by the boy's actions, Holden walks up a hill to speak to the hostile leaders who are lined up (Hollywood style) ready to charge the mission and slaughter all of its defenders. Refusing to hear the words of the missionary, Kamiakin (Michael Ansara) shoots Holden before he can utter a word; in turn, a Christian Indian kills Kamiakin. Now the true climactic element of the film is played out, as the hero of the film, First Sergeant Emmett Bell (Jeff Chandler, no longer sporting his Chiricahua mane and headband), proceeds to dress down the Christian Indians for allowing Kamiakin to seduce them and sit on their horses watching in silence as their leader killed the Christ-like Holden. Bell challenges the Christian Indians to re-adopt their "animal" Indian names and to go back to living as the wild beasts their names represented before Holden brought them *his* god. Like whipped curs, they walk down the hill to the mission with their heads down and their tails between their legs. Two strong American figures, Holden and Bell, forced the Indians to understand the greatness of the Christian god, and in turn, the superiority of American culture.

Other directors found Delmer Daves' "good Indian" formula to their liking, including the master himself. In *Pony Soldier* (1952), Joseph Newman uses the backdrop the Sitting Bull's post-Little Big Horn escape into Canada to show the Northern Cree of Chief Standing Bear (Stuart Randall) as friends of whites. Chief Standing Bear's tribe assist Royal Mounted Police Constable Duncan MacDonald (Tyrone Power) rescue American hostages taken by Sitting Bull's Sioux, but only after MacDonald kills the young Cree warrior Konah (Cameron Mitchell), who wants his people to join the hostiles from the United States.

Director George Marshall reduced his budget on *The Savage* (1953), by making the white hero and the "good Indian" the same person. Eleven-year old Jim Aherne (Charlton Heston) is the sole survivor of a Crow attack on white settlers. In awe of his resistance against his people's enemies (regardless of their age, Indians are in awe of any white male who stands against overwhelming odds), the Sioux Chief, Yellow Eagle adopts him into his tribe and renames him War Bonnet. When war between the Sioux and Americans breaks out, War Bonnet must chose.

War Bonnet will vacillate back and forth between his white origins and adopted Sioux upbringing. In the end he betrays his Indian friends, but only to bring peace between the two people. After sabotaging a Sioux ambush of white settlers War Bonnet returns to his Sioux village to explain his behavior to his people. During his speech an angered warrior will launch a lance at War Bonnet. Paternal instinct will cause Yellow Eagle rush to his adopted son's side, despite the young man's betrayal. War Bonnet survives his wounds and is taken by his Sioux father to the soldier's fort. When War Bonnet, now Jim Aherne, enters the fort, the audience is assured this honorable man will bring peace between the two sides.

Delmer Daves also successfully reused his old "good Indian" formula in another western, *Drum Beat* (1954). "Good Indian" Manok (Anthony Caruso), his sister, Toby (Marissa Pavan), and their white friend Johnny MacKay (Alan Ladd) bring an end to the Modoc War of 1872-1873. Unlike the charismatic and independent Cochise in *Broken Arrow*, this Daves' "good Indian" meekly follows his white hero, unable to foster any backbone to stand up against the menacing Captain Jack (Charles Bronson), leader of the hostile Modocs. After the Indian maiden, Toby, sacrifices her life to rescue him, MacKay captures Captain Jack. Before being executed for the murder of General Edward

Canby (Warner Anderson), Captain Jack addresses his captor, Johnny MacKay. His comments to MacKay help morph this once enemy of the white man into a more masculine "good Indian" comrade to MacKay, than the passive Manok, "If when Captain Jack goes to the Happy Hunting Grounds, he finds out no white people are allowed, I tell them to let in my good friend, Johnny!" The audience sees an Indian who even in the face of death begrudgingly recognizes the superiority of his white rival. In the theaters, and later on television, these films helped form the images of Indians that a generation of young Americans could feel compassion for, yet still recognize their subservient role to the superior white male hero.

These few films are but a small cross-section of the "Childhood Indian" films that influenced my formative years, and although one can argue that they are merely film depictions and are meant for nothing more than the commercial entertainment of an audience, these works are far more powerful than the public imagines. Much of the imagery that literature, film, and television have employed to identify Native culture has emphasized socially unacceptable, even depraved, behavior. Having laid out a concept that the aforementioned mediums disseminate unfavorable impressions of Natives, and record the social mores and sentiments of the nation, it is only natural that even the most zealous pro-Indian film of the 1950s will keep alive the most critical elements of the American mythos, and the subsidiary role Natives played in the nation's perceived history. The wide range of Indian film and television brought to me as a child represent the socio-political icons the country needed at various moments in time to energize the contemporary ideology then fashioning American society. As ideology changed so to did the depiction of Indians, but the Indian of the next generation of films will show that not much really does change.

ENDNOTES CHAPTER 4

[1] The use of the term "Great Father" is of course in reference to the distinguished Father Francis Paul Prucha's commodious research of United States paternalistic attempts to aid Natives, while in fact doing nothing more than forcing a more dependent relationship by Natives on the federal government. This chapter argues that cinematic Indian images are a popular culture extension of government Indian policy maker's rationale suggesting Native backwardness that necessitated paternalistic intervention on the part of U.S. officials to manage Native affairs.

[2] Clifford Trafzer, *As Long as the Grass Shall Grow and Rivers Flow*, Fort Worth, Texas: Harcourt College Publishers, (2000), 115-116.

[3] Albert Memmi, *The Colonizer and the Colonized*, New York: The Orion Press, (1957), 79.

[4] Rebecca Kugel, *To Be the Main Leader of Our People: A History of Minnesota Ojibwe Politics, 1825-1898*, East Lansing: Michigan State University Press, (1998), 30-32.

[5] Kugel, 21.

[6] Ironically, the prime architect of President Grant's Peace Policy was Commissioner of Indian Affairs Ely S. Parker, the Seneca who was the first Native American to hold this post. See "The Peace Policy" in Francis Paul Prucha's *The Great White Father: The United States Government and the American Indians*, Lincoln: University of Nebraska Press, (1984).

[7] Christine Bolt, *American Indian Policy and American Reform: Case Studies of the Campaign to Assimilate the*

American Indian, London: Allen & Unwin, (1987), 75-76.

[8] Bolt, 80.

[9] Vine Deloria, Jr., "The Indian Rights Association," *The Aggressions of Civilization: Federal Indian Policy Since the 1880s*, edited by Sandra L. Cadwalader and Vine Deloria, Jr., Philadelphia: Temple University Press, (1984), 6.

[10] H. Henrietta Stockel, *Survival of the Spirit: Chiricahua Apaches in Captivity*, Reno: University of Nevada Press, (1993), 125.

[11] Stockel, 298.

[12] Ibid.

[13] Frederick E. Hoxie, *A Final Compromise: The Campaign to Assimilate the Indians, 1880-1920*, Lincoln: University of Nebraska Press, (1984), 160.

[14] Hoxie, 77.

[15] Brian Dippie, *The Vanishing American: White Attitudes and U.S. Indian Policy*, Middletown, Connecticut: Wesleyan University Press, (1982), 307.

[16] Dippie, 231.

[17] Dippie, 319.

[18] Kenneth R. Philp, *John Collier's Crusade for Indian Reform, 1920-1954*, Tucson: The University of Arizona Press, (1977), 165.

[19] Thomas Biolsi, *Organizing the Lakota: The Political Economy of the New Deal on the Pine Ridge and Rosebud Reservations*, Tucson: The University of Arizona Press, (1998) c1992, 115.

[20] Sally L. Jones, "The First but Not the Last of the 'Vanishing Indian': Edwin Forrest and Mythic Re-creations of the Native Population," *Dressing in Feathers: The Construction of the Indian in American Popular Culture*, edited by S. Elizabeth Bird, Boulder, Colorado: Westview Press, (1996), 13.

[21] Ralph and Natasha Friar, *The Only Good Indian...The Hollywood Gospel*, New York: Drama Book Specialist/Publishers, (1972), 202.

[22] One of the most persistent arguments defending European and American imperialism has been the concept that people of color are incapable to appreciate democracy and all its enduring principles: freedom, liberty, and equality. Only after an extended exposure to democracy (White culture), either through the forced occupation of the Natives homeland, or education in the colonizer's mother country, are the Natives able to grasp a limited understanding of the political system. See Stuart Creigton Miller's *Benevolent Assimilation* (1982) to examine an 1890s American application of this belief in regards to Filipino independence.

[23] James Stewart's Jeffords will become proficient enough in Apache that Daves is able to depict all dialogue between Jeffords and the Chiricahuas in English for the benefit of the audience.

[24] In his extensively researched analysis of the Frontier Myth in America in *Gunfighter Nation* (1992) Richard Slotkin identifies the literary and historical White

frontiersman whom becomes so proficient with Native American culture he out-Indians the Indians.

[25] A critical moment in the story occurs when the Chiricahua are recognizing the coming of age ceremony of a young maiden. Jeffords makes reference to fact that he understands the maiden currently holds the same metaphysical power as White Painted Woman, the most revered Apache deity. Part of the "Man Who Knows Indians" mystique is their ability to apply their knowledge of Native beliefs to meet the needs of the White man. Cochise shows a look of astonishment that Jeffords knows of White Painted Woman. An impressed Cochise tells Jeffords, "No White man has ever taken the time to know our customs:" it is clear that at this point Jeffords now holds the negotiating upper hand.

[26] During the Apache wars of the 1880s, Geronimo maintained a strong friendship, and was allied with Cochise's youngest son, Naiche. In a series interviews conducted during the 1940s with ethno historian Eve Ball, Nedni Apache elder Asa Daklugie described Chiricahua alliances in the 1860s between Cochise, Mangas Coloradas, and Juh that would preclude any notion of intertribal rivalries, including those of sub-leaders such as Geronimo. Therefore, the films depiction of Geronimo's defiance of Cochise's peace agreement with the Americans is merely one more example of Hollywood's artistic license. In addition, by the early-1870s, the period *Broken Arrow* takes place; most Chiricahuas still harbored a very strong hatred of Mexicans, and had yet to develop the kind of hatred for Americans warranting any animated disapproval of peace treaties with the United States.

[27] According to Cochise, the death of Sonseeahray is used as the reference point by which the two sides must work harder to maintain peace in the face of stiff

opposition from both sides. However at a more subliminal, and perhaps sacred, level Jeffords' marriage to an Indian cannot reach fruition. The mix-blood relationship between a White man and Indian women was unacceptable to a post World War II America. Thus even in a film claiming to depict Indians in a respectful manner, the time-honored American abhorrence to miscegenation prevented Jeffords from living "happily ever after" with his Indian "'squaw."

[28] Memmi, 154.

[29] See Richard Drinnon's "The Secret Agent: Edward Geary Lansdale," in *Facing West.*

[30] David Theo Goldberg, *Racist Culture: Philosophy and the Politics of Meaning*, Oxford: Blackwell Publishers, (1993), 118-119.

[31] From the soundtrack of the film *Sitting Bull* (1954), directed by Sidney Salkow and Rene Cardona.

[32] The fight with Crazy Horse is itself a feature of the White/Indian mythos. Parrish rode into the Sioux village alone and questioned the manliness of the Sioux when Sitting Bull orders Parrish's release so that the women can kill him. When the belligerently portrayed Crazy Horse stands up for the pride of the men in the village the knife duel is arranged, of course Parrish out-Indians the Indian and defeats his rival in an Indian skill. For the myth's sake, more importantly, Parrish spares the life of his conquered foe. Natives are worthless enough that in single combat their blood isn't even worth spilling.

[33] Sam was an African American who had lived most of his life with the Sioux. When asked by Parrish if he spoke English Sam said, "No." Confused that this man

was answering his questions as if he did understand Parrish asked Sam what it was then that he was speaking. Sam replied, "I'm speaking Long Knives." Parrish was able to make a difference for not only Indians, but also African Americans. In addition to rescuing the Indians from annihilation, Parrish will help civilize Sam, the Black-Indian.

[34] Nicholas Thomas, *Colonialism's Culture: Anthropology, Travel and Government* Princeton: Princeton University, (1994), 45.

[35] Memmi, 151.

[36] Thomas Gladwin with the collaboration of Ahmad Saidin, *Slaves of the White Myth: The Psychology of Neocolonialism*, Atlantic Highlands, New Jersey: Humanities Press, (1980).

Chapter 5
Serving the Nation Proudly:
The Allegorical Indian, the Cold War, Civil Rights
And the Vietnam War.

An enigmatic use of film Indians ran concurrent with the paternalistic Indians of the 1950s and continues to thrive in these days of a multicultural and diversity-filled America. This use is an image that transcends both the aforementioned colonizer mentality and the paternalistic Indians. These allegorical Indians are far more complex to understand due to the nature of their purported use. While these cinematic images maintain the traditional characterizations from both of the Indian categories already analyzed, this variation carries a specific meaning that re-defines the context of the White (sub)Conscience. These are Indian representations that become specific metaphors for a political or social movement.

Sometimes reflecting the negative stereotypes of the colonizer mind or instead depicting the White-dependent noble savage, the context of allegorical Indian films relayed a second level of indoctrination meant to influence the audience's opinion one way or another. Hollywood possesses an effect public relations machine that has the ability to sway the minds of viewers from all walks of life, and all parts of the globe. The tentacles of its influence are impressive. As cinema studies scholar Toby Miller argues, Hollywood's hegemonic control of the global film industry stems from a well-organized and relentless barrage of U.S. "cultural imperialism" that crushes international productions in their own national markets.[1] Although Miller's concept of a "Global Hollywood" emphasizes a capitalist-driven Hollywood domination of global cinema markets, the essential factor creating this situation is American cinema's ability to deliver a story, regardless of its plausibility, rich in visual context. Film represents the essence of what the audience wants to believe is reality; not necessarily because it is true, but because cinema embodies the characteristics in specific roles that will suggest a hierarchical social power base founded on racial and gender representations.[2] This chapter will focus on the racial representations found in these films.

It comes as no surprise that the cinematic Indians of the colonizer mentality and paternalistic "good Indian" films suggest this very principle. Either as the hostile vermin necessitating extermination at the hands of the valiant frontiersman, or as the ingenuous and dependent sidekick of the altruistic and benevolent white father figure, the Indian provides the perfect antithesis of the intelligent, virile and morally superior and politically dominant American. With this ideological framework Hollywood filmmakers, given the opportunity to develop their social or political cinematic allegory, replicated whichever image of the Indians best met their needs.

During the last half of the twentieth century American audiences have been exposed to these Indian images in a contextual form that develops the character beyond the traditional descriptions examined earlier in this work. Although a metaphorically more complex Indian appears on the screen to express contemporary issues of significance, the imperative White (sub)Conscience stereotypes are maintained. The viewer is thus inculcated with a dual set of issues to absorb into the socio-political influencing White (sub)Conscience. Although both Indian images thrived in Hollywood through my critical "Childhood Indian" years that end in the mid-1970s, I will examine these film strategies separately, rather than combining the two cinematic techniques.

American Studies scholar Richard Slotkin describes the twenty-five year period between 1948-1972 as the Golden Age of the Western.[3] Within the metaphoric context of the Cold War, it is not by coincidence that the strongest anti-Indian image portrayal occurred during the most turbulent phase of the Cold War. In Slotkin's reinterpretation of Native American images during the early stages of the Cold War, 1946- 1954, he explains that the "savage" Indian becomes the metaphoric representation of the Red; a Communist horde poised to strike at the heart of Western Civilization, capitalism, and the wholesome qualities that the United States stood for.[4]

Classic "Childhood Indian" westerns, such as *Rio Grande* (1949), *The Last Outpost* (1951), *Arrowhead* (1953), and *Dakota Incident* (1956) persisted in using the negative Indian imagery that lifts the simple entertainment value of the film to a level of political allegory. In the Cold War uncertainties of the post-World War II world, Hollywood recycled menacing Indians of the colonizer mentality to represent the new threat to civilization. It fell upon the Cold War Hollywood Indian to personify the Communist machinations of global domination and thus to warn the American audience of the serious menace posed to the civilized world.

Because a society's very existence was at risk, the need to protect that society from the threat allowed for extreme measures. The Cold War western becomes the cinematic vessel for understanding the conservative, even reactionary, nature of the American politics during this period. No film of this era demonstrates this proxy image of the Indian better than John Ford's *Rio Grande* (1949). For the Indian to make his/her cinematic transition the context in which he/she is viewed must first occur. *Rio Grande* offers the most complex examples of the western as Cold War metaphor. As Slotkin so eloquently explains,

> *Rio Grande* develops to the extreme the logic inherent in the combat films representation of the platoon as a metaphoric "America." Here metaphor becomes

metonymy. The cavalry is not merely a 'representation' of American democracy—the agent of its policy, the metaphoric expression of its values. Democracy and nation are now entirely identified with the military. Cavalry ideology incorporates and assigns a proper place to all the significant characters of the western landscape, Indians and Whites, man and woman, outlaw and law-bringer.

The major socio-political debates of the time have been conveniently symbolized under a Cold War metaphor within the context of age-old struggle between the civilized whites and savage Indians (Reds). Slotkin further explains the parameters of social interaction the characters establish, and grant consent for the harsh political decisions to come as a result of the Cold War,

Cavalry codes and practices provide sure guides to the resolution of every ideological opposition: democracy vs. authority; civilian vs. soldier; egalitarian vs. hierarchy; justice vs. law; civilization vs. savagery.... *Rio Grande* also develops the political implications of this identification. If the cavalry subsumes "democracy," then the rules that govern the cavalry are indistinguishable from the ideological imperatives of democracy. Therefore we must consent to the replacement of traditional or "civilian" codes and practices by the military principles of doing whatever is necessary to complete our mission—even when the mission is so questionable [it] has to be a "Mission with No Record."[5]

When Lt. Colonel Kirby York (John Wayne) leads a detachment of U. S. Cavalry into Mexico, violating Mexican sovereignty, to rescue White children captured by hostile Apaches, the mission is a necessary consequence of the dire circumstances. The "Mission with No Record" into Mexico helped return Americans to safety while restoring order to the social fabric of American frontier. The Apaches (Reds) are identified as monolithic drunken males (No Native women ever appear in the film), displaying their hedonistic behavior in front of a church, God's house of worship. Like the atheist Soviet horde that blasphemes against God with its communist schemes and disregard for civilized people, the only solution to the Apache threat is to annihilate the source before it can strike. A pre-emptive attack against unsuspecting Apaches could not be described as uncivilized, because in the context of a Cold War America fearful of a Soviet attack against the United States, the nation's security necessitated these actions.

Within this cloak and dagger political atmosphere, cinema's media brethren, the press, was generating a propaganda campaign that served as public relations guides to U.S. State foreign policy in Third World counties. *Life*, *Time*, *Newsweek* and *The New York Times* offered up articles depicting nationalist leaders such as Iranian Prime Minister Muhammad Musaddiq as a childlike religious fanatic after he nationalized the British oil interests in his country that had been reaping immense profits without compensating Iran sufficiently. As the Central Intelligence Agency (CIA) was covertly undermining the authority of Musaddiq in order to supplant him with the pro-American figure, Shah Mohammad Reza Pahlevi, these periodicals ran stories suggesting the danger Musaddiq proved to American security. Musaddiq's behavior, it was argued, emboldened Soviet aggression; U. S. officials who refused to act decisively also came under attack.[6]

On August 19, 1953 the CIA rid Americans of this problematic character. Musaddiq was overthrown after CIA money was spent to destabilize his government. The pro-American Shah replaced the nationalist Musaddiq, whom Americans feared as a potential Soviet dupe. Although it is difficult to implicate the American press in the CIA's activities in Iran, it did help create the image of Musaddiq that generated a public response denouncing any criticism of the State Department's involvement in the internal politics of a foreign country. The media discourse on Iran helped create what sociologist John Foran describes as the "structure of feeling" that necessitated the coup.[7]

Within this "structure of feeling" context, there is little wonder that even children became commercial targets of anti-communist propaganda. In 1951, the Children's Crusade Against Communism, a series of children's bubblegum cards, warned of the communist threat. Depicting the figures or scenes identified with the communist menace, the cards gave a healthy lesson on the goals and results of Red aggression. The back of one card titled *War-Maker* described Mao Zedong as a man who "delights in war," and who claims history "is written in blood and iron." The passage concludes that, "the free world must find a way to keep war-makers like Mao Tse-tung [sic] from shedding the blood of innocent people."[8]

Even more ominous than the cards identifying the leaders of the communist struggle were those depicting the results of the movement. In *Olga and Ivan*, children learned in terrifying details the fear the average Soviet citizen lived in, "A knock at the door— and the typical Russian family fears the worst" introduced the grim life of a Soviet family. The narrative continued, "They are told where to work…their daily routine insists on absolute obedience to their leaders and following Communist doctrine." To reinforce the deprived state of these people the concluding commentary claimed, "A simple anti-communist remark by anyone of them could result in a visit from the police…. Prison without fair trial or appeal faces all. This is life under Communism!"[9]

144

These brief sketches left little to the imagination. Americans must act aggressively or fall prey to the totalitarian state *War-Makers* like Mao or Josef Stalin already had established in their countries. The United States was in the midst of a full-blown Red Scare; Hollywood was up to the task and was not to be left behind. Newspapers, magazines and even children's bubblegum cards conveyed the socio-political emotions of a nation locked in a struggle for its very existence.

The Cold War called for extreme measures; Americans needed stability to counter the Red threat. The classic Indian trope of civilization defeating savagery became socially irrelevant, or more specifically, needed to develop into a contemporary, more contextual, allegory. The battle still needed to be waged against savagism; but a new image was needed that was capable of depicting the much more sinister creature that was lurking in the foliage. Without its Indian metaphor the nation was unable to contrast White, civilized progress (democracy) against Native, primitive disorder. The current threat to the American way of life, embodying the newest form of primitive disorder, was communism. Therefore, although the "old order" Indian was socially anachronistic (and being redeveloped for its "innovative" paternalistic Indian of the 1950s), the Cold War Indian image was vital in the battle, "...involving the fulfillment or destruction not only of this Republic but of civilization itself."[10] The Indian as a symbolic opponent sustained enough metaphoric social value to become a Hollywood symbol of communism during the Cold War.[11]

The man largely given credit for winning the Cold War and destroying the Soviet Union, Ronald Reagan, addressed this issue in his previous career as an actor in the film *The Last Outpost* (1951). Two Civil War brothers on opposite sides of the conflict must decide how to defend a town against hostile Apaches. Their personal differences provide director Lewis R.

Foster with the ideal backdrop to communicate his Cold War allegory. At odds with his Union brother Colonel Jeb Britton (Bruce Bennett), the Confederate officer Captain Vance Britten (Ronald Reagan) explains to northern supporter Julie McQuade (Rhonda Fleming) that it is imperative that he and his Yankee brother forget their differences in the face of overwhelming Apache numbers.

Britten firmly states to the naïve McQuade that if they do not forget their differences the Apaches will wipe out all Whites, Union or Confederate. In the language of the Cold War the message is plain: as Liberal or Conservative all Americans must stand together against the "Red" threat. Released during the Cold War tension fueled Korean conflict, *The Last Outpost* expressed the danger a divided nation posed to all Americans in its struggle against the Soviet Union. Needless to say, the two warring brothers set aside their political rivalries to rescue the besieged town when they led a spectacular unified cavalry charge[12] against their Red tormentors.

People such as the naïve Julie McQuade played a critical role in depicting the dangers of communism. People unable to understand the far reaches of the Red Menace posed as much of a threat to the safety of civilization as did the actual danger. President Harry S. Truman's secretary of state Dean Acheson led an influential element within the government that held firmly to the principles of a National Security Council top-secret document that was written in response to increased pressure on Truman's apparently soft stance on the Communists. Authored by Cold War authority Paul Nitze in April, 1950 National Security Council Paper Sixty-Eight (NSC-68) became the blue print for American Cold War policies.

In its essence, NSC-68 called for a hard-line approach to Soviet aspirations to global domination. Acheson was "determined to launch a global offensive to

146

reclaim the initiative in the Cold War and to shut up critics at home."[13] Negotiating with the Reds had been a grave mistake, Truman had been accused of being too soft on communism, and Acheson, with Truman's consent, insisted on a new hard-line approach.[14] The fall of China to the Communists, and the Soviet detonation of an atomic device in 1949 placed the U.S. on the defensive. As American studies scholars Richard Drinnon and Richard Slotkin argue, the United States found itself threatened by a "Red" menace. According to the two men, much like Americans had done during the nineteenth century when the nation was instigating a war with Mexico and exterminating Native populations during westward expansion, this generation of Americans was producing a new danger to its existence that would call for self-defense measures.

Two westerns depicting the essential principle incorporated into the NSC-68 doctrine of victimized Americans defending themselves against the overwhelming odds trope were *Arrowhead* (1953) and *Dakota Incident* (1956). Richard Drinnon further developed Herman Melville's "Metaphysics of Indian-hating" concept to explain a national ideology claiming self-defense from Indian depredations. According to Drinnon, when Americans exterminated scores of Natives the rationale claimed it was done only as a last resort to fend off the Indian attacks. Each of the two films mentioned masterfully craft the timeless American myth of beleaguered victim within the concept of Cold War discourse.

Film viewers were treated to a western that maintained time-honored images of both Whites and Indians, thus making the interwoven Cold War narrative appear less of an element of propaganda and more of a reality. As mentioned in an earlier chapter, film historian Ray B. Browne argues film has a mesmerizing affect on the viewer that leaves a subliminal impression on the individual. Whether one is willing to admit it or not, he/she does believe the context of the characters and narrative in a film, regardless of one's knowledge that the work is strictly fantasy.[15] This gives the films their power.

Longtime British Broadcasting Company producer/critic Phillip French called the 1953 western *Arrowhead*,

> An ultra-right-wing allegory of the McCarthy period in which the Indians...do service for the Communists, and the whites, with their unwavering leader Bannon, for those red-blooded American patriots bent on rooting out the Communist conspiracy at home and standing up to its menace abroad.[16]

French's ideological criticism of the film is well warranted, although he fails to explain the actual metaphoric imagery that the director Charles Marquis Warren employed in the storyline. Warren developed the Cold War allegory by using a raw and unbridled racist narrative. *Arrowhead*'s lead character Ed Bannon (Charlton Heston) was raised as a child amongst the Chiricahua Apaches. Although the film never explains the origins of Bannon's Apache odyssey, suffice to say he was a model "Man Who Knows Indians."

Bannon's experience with the Apaches molded a realistic (according to Warren) appreciation for the sadistic nature of these people.[17] Two separate discussions between Bannon and army officers set the tone for the film. After "Chief of Scouts" Bannon kills three Apaches he claimed were on the warpath, his commanding officer, Colonel Weybright (Lewis Martin), chastises him for botching up a planned peace settlement. When told by Weybright that the Apaches and Americans had negotiated an agreement and that the Indians were coming in to surrender, Bannon calmly responds, "These are Apaches you're dealing with." Needless to say, any belief the viewer held that Indians negotiated in good faith was removed when the "Man Who Knows Indians" explained the true nature of these people. When the Colonel asks an Indian scout to confirm a Bannon explanation of Apache customs the scout claims, "It's not for me to say, I'm no longer a savage." Bannon quickly retorts a cynical, "Yeah."

Bannon has clearly identified to the audience that the Colonel is naïve to believe that the Apaches can be trusted. Just as importantly, he has shown that Indians never change, even when they claim to be on the side of the Americans. After a burial detail is assigned to bury the dead Indians, Bannon warns the Colonel to take a different route to the fort than he had planned. Bannon, the expert, is certain the Apache are up to no good. The Colonel refuses his advice, and will pay for his blunder.

As Bannon and Captain Bill North (Brian Keith) discuss the killing incident while the Indians are being buried, the officer tells the scout, "Azunni (The Apache Chief) gave his word he'd come in today." "You're as blind as the Colonel..." responds Bannon. North continues, "If you keep on hating Apaches, we'll be digging one of those for you (a grave)." Bannon proceeds to calmly explain to North, "I don't hate them, I know them." The warning to the viewer is obvious, an individual who maintains a hard-line approach to the Soviet Union does not necessarily do so from an irrationally influenced emotion.

Experienced knowledge of the "other" suggests that appeasement of the Communists will only lead to defeat. Anyone believing the Reds were willing to negotiate fairly with the United States is a fool. The Cold War-era "Man Who Knows Indians" understands the treacherous nature of the Communist and must be allowed to formulate anti-communist policy. When the Apaches launch an ambush of the Colonel's detachment, exactly where Bannon had predicted they would attack, the viewer is reminded why the experts must be allowed to handle the Red threat. Trusting the Reds will only lead to defeat.

During the remainder of the film Bannon must continue to battle those people believing the most dangerous of the Apaches, the Chiricahua, are serious about making peace with the United States. Needless to say, Bannon is convinced otherwise. Before dying from wounds received in the Apache ambush Colonel Weybright fires Bannon. The new "Chief of Scouts," Jerry August (Jim Anderson) maintains the same naïve belief of his superiors that, if dealt with honestly, the Chiricahua will make peace with the Whites.

The leader of the Chiricahua is the messianic figure Toriano (Jack Palance) who returns from an eastern Indian school. According to the whites, he is therefore an educated Indian. Like the Indian scout claiming he is no longer a savage, the Toriano figure with his Indian school education, indicative of liberal America's attempt to convert the Indian, represents the clandestine enemy. To the Whites, both Toriano and the Apache scout claim to have accepted the way of the "White Man," but deep inside they are still Indian, and cannot be trusted. Similarly, Americans must be careful that the Communists have also not infiltrated their society. When *Arrowhead* was released in 1953 considerable mistrust and anxiety permeated American society. The nation was in the last stages of the infamous McCarthy Hearings, the House Un-American Activities Committee's (HUAC) investigations of Hollywood, labor, and the State Department contributed to this tension. *Arrowhead* made those fears seem acceptable. Cold War cultural expert Tom Englehardt explained the essential 1950s American paranoia, " Communists were 'termites boring from within.' They were 'Moscow masters of deceit,' of 'mirage' and 'disguise.'"[18]

Arrowhead suggested Cold War fears of Communist infiltration were well warranted. The Indian "master of deceit" struck when the Americans were most vulnerable. The climactic ending of the film begins with the betrayal of Jim Eagle (Pat Hogan), the "un-savaged" Apache scout, at Toriano's surrender to an American cavalry column. Toriano and Jim Eagle have fooled "Chief of Scouts" Jerry August, costing the white scout his life. They were ready to massacre the survivors of the treachery until Bannon uses smoke signals to trick Toriano into thinking his scouts were warning him of cavalry reinforcements. Although he had been fired, and was despised by the soldiers, Bannon acts on his conscience and risks his life to save the besieged troop.

If the United States is to win the Cold War it must not allow itself the luxury of trusting the Communists. Americans must allow their best Cold Warriors, despite any distasteful flaws, to combat the deceitful Communist horde. In the end, Bannon kills his Indian foe and exposes the self-proclaimed "Chosen One" as a fraud to his followers. Two critical features of the White (sub)Conscience are depicted in this ending. The first maintains the element of white physical superiority. Bannon breaks Toriano's back in a hand-to-hand duel. The second element occurs when Bannon tells the new leader of the Chiricahua to take his people home and to forget about Toriano's dream of Apache self-determination.[19] Beaten and dejected the Indians meekly turn their horses back home, apparently thankful for the paternalistic White man's benevolent gesture. Bannon's benevolence comes only after his defeat of Toriano. Despite his actions one is assured that the ex-scout's opinion of Apaches has not changed. Bannon handles the Indian uprising in the most expedient and efficient manner possible. No negotiations between American diplomats and Red representatives were necessary. The Indians need only obey the word of the "Man Who Knows Indians" (Cold War expert) to receive justice.

151

The question of negotiating with the Communists proved a controversial issue for Cold War experts. An example of the serious nature of this issue is Cold War diplomat George Kennan's 8,000-word telegram, simply referred to as the "Long Telegram," that first introduced the term that will become the foundation of Cold War policy: containment. The following year an article credited to a Mr. X, published in the July issue *Foreign Affairs*, that all who had read the "Long Telegram" knew was penned by Kennan, reiterated the essence of containment. It called for the United States to adopt a stance towards the Soviet Union requiring Americans to be "long-term patient but firm and vigilant application of Russian expansive tendencies...."[20] The crucial understanding of containment was that the United States was not to engage the Soviet Union in negotiation. According to Kennan only force could bring the Soviet Union to its knees and end the Communist threat.

The film *Dakota Incident* (1956) recognized this danger of negotiation with the Reds and the need to maintain a firm hand against the Communist foe. Using as its backdrop the familiar besieged frontier family trope, *Dakota Incident* contrasts the polarized strategies that factions within the heroic party employed against their Indian attackers. Despite the warning that the Sioux were on the warpath, a stagecoach full of a cross-section of American archetypes headed off on its ominous journey. Unlike John Ford's *Stagecoach,* the Indian presence is not the foreboding figure lurking in the background that aided in the suspense of the film. In *Dakota Incident* the Indian makes his presence felt midway through the movie and remains a threat to the film's conclusion.

Chased by the Sioux the stagecoach overturns and the passengers are forced to take cover in a shallow ravine. Here the Cold War drama is developed. Amongst the passengers is an eastern-bred U.S. senator named Blakely (Ward Bond). A pompous and vain individual, Senator Blakely adheres to a belief that the government must adopt a policy of appeasement and negotiation with the Indians. Although frontier residents remind Blakely of numerous Indian depredations against innocent White settlers, the Senator remains convinced that the savages could be brought around to recognize and respect peace.

In contrast to the misguided Blakely is the stern and fair-minded gunfighter John Banner (Dale Robertson). Banner identified himself early in the film as just when he refuses to kill a man, later identified as his brother, in a gunfight. Although he does force the man to walk unarmed into the dangerous wilderness, he will not be his own brother's executioner. During the siege in the ravine Banner displays his leadership by calming the nerves of the frightened passengers while coolly picking off Indians who foolishly expose themselves to his fire.

The rivalry between Senator Blakely and John Banner to determine the future of the passengers illuminates the dynamics of Cold War politics. The highbrow Blakely represents the Liberal Democrats, men Kennan feared took too soft a negotiation stance with the Soviet Union. Throughout the struggle at the ravine Blakely's true character is exposed. Even in self-defense he refuses to fire a weapon; under severe water restrictions he sneaks a drink when no one is watching. Perhaps his most depraved act, as the small party was facing death was that he made a sexual advance on the sleeping, buxom Amy Clark (Linda Darnell). Banner rescues Clark from Blakely's unsolicited advances and firmly establishes himself as the dominant male in the party.

Clearly humiliated by his aborted romantic escapade, Blakely will be challenged to defend his principles. Clark angrily accuses Blakely of being an unethical and weak-willed person incapable of upholding his own convictions. Blakely scavenges up enough strength to leave the safety of the ravine to offer a dialogue with the Indians. As Blakely opens his arms and shouts out, "I come to speak peace with my Red brothers," a pair of Indian arrows put an abrupt end to the negotiations. Blakely's death is a reminder to the viewer that negotiating with the Reds is impossible. The enemy knows only force; Banner's resolute defense of the ravine eventually reduces the Indians to only their leader. Thirsty and alone, the man humbly enters the ravine asking for water. Force has convinced this Indian to seek peace, but more importantly, those peace concessions came at the discretion of the victorious American.

The hard-line Cold War policies of NSC-68, George Kennan, Dean Acheson and countless other "Cold Warriors" were delivered through the American mass media and popular culture of the 1950s, and Hollywood Indians played their patriotic roles in countless westerns such as these described in this chapter. Two generations of children were given their Cold War indoctrination by these films, one during their initial 1950s theater release, and a second later in reruns on television to the children of the 1960's and '70s.

The allegorical Indian of the Cold War gave way to a pair of images that marked the divisive and volatile social atmosphere of the 1960s. Ironically two sides of the same social coin imparted their unique Indian characterizations. In the first instance, Liberal Hollywood sought to make a serious statement in support of civil rights, but did little more than place the Indian in the narrative background of these dramas. Films such as *Sergeant Rutledge* (1960) acted as a vehicle for Hollywood to demonstrate its commitment to African American racial equality. Sadly, Hollywood films that praised Blacks as worthy of civil rights, still saw the Indian as the social outsider, the enemy that Blacks and whites would now join to fight together.

As the Vietnam War grew controversial and vied with the Civil Rights Movement for public attention, the second representation morphed the background Indian of the civil rights westerns into an allegoric re-design of the 1950s Cold War western. Only this time the stories carried a distinctly anti-war message. Within the socio-political context of the Vietnam era, cinematic Indians once again were metaphors in such films as the 1970s *Soldier Blue* (1970). Like its Cold War counterpart, the Vietnam era Indian was used to convey a political agenda to the viewer. This Indian represented a political metaphor opposite that of the Cold War Indian, yet like its predecessor, the Vietnam era Indian served to represent an "other," rather a real Native. These last of the "Childhood Indians" served to act as transitional characterizations that would change the way Indians could be depicted on film.

Sergeant Rutledge was my first introduction to the Black western hero. This "Childhood Indian" film was my first lesson on the famous exploits of the all African American 9th and 10th Cavalry Regiments, the Buffalo Soldiers, that helped defeat Natives during the Indian wars of the late-nineteenth century. John Ford was interested enough in civil rights to make a film about these long forgotten American heroes that also taught the viewer a lesson on the wastefulness of racial bigotry.

Directed by the iconic western film director John Ford, *Sergeant Rutledge* uses an Apache uprising as a backdrop to explore the complex understanding of changing race relations in the United States during the late-1950s. The Civil Rights Movement created a social firestorm that tested the character of the nation. Although in 1954 the United States Supreme Court had ruled 9-0 to end segregation in public accommodations, apathetic support from the north and downright resistance in the south made desegregation a difficult struggle for African Americans. Ford sought to raise

155

awareness of the need to recognize the Civil Rights of African Americans through the film *Sergeant Rutledge*. As he did in his 1939 western classic *Stagecoach*, Ford used metaphoric characters to depict his social allegory. In both cases significantly the Indian serves only to add suspense to the narrative.

Sergeant Rutledge tells the story of an African American soldier, 1st Sergeant Braxton Rutledge (Woody Strode), accused of the murder of a White girl. To find the truth to her death, Ford intersperses the trial of Rutledge with flashbacks of events occurring the night of the girl's death and in the days that followed, including a series of Apache attacks on White settlers. Various characters are present at Rutledge's trial, including upstanding women of the community who can't understand how Rutledge could kill the girl. In the socially accepted trope present in American literature from when the first captivity-narratives were published in the United States, there *is* an inherent malevolence within Blacks ready to strike Whites without notice, therefore the women display a tacit acceptance of the sergeant's guilt.[21]

The legal posturing between the prosecuting attorney and Rutledge's defense lawyer acted out the social debate absorbing the nation during the late-1950s. The prosecutor, with his genteel southern arrogance, Captain Shattuck (Carleton Young) strongly emphasizes Rutledge's race to support circumstantial evidence of his guilt. The northern defense attorney Lieutenant Tom Cantrell (Jeffrey Hunter) counters Shattuck at every stage of the trial, trying to convince the court his client has proven himself a "credit to his race," at one point actually rescuing a White woman from hostile Apaches. When a White man is exposed as the actual rapist and murderer of the girl, the audience realizes that traditional racist beliefs had almost allowed an innocent man to die for a crime he did not commit.

156

In depicting Rutledge's trial as one of archaic narrow-minded principles of racism versus those of a law-abiding, race-tolerant society, the viewer is reminded of the struggle for racial equality being fought in the American south at that very moment. Ford displayed his American spirit and played his civic part in supporting Civil Rights. The irony of Ford's cinematic work is that, even within the context of the Civil Rights Movement, the director's Indians were relegated to the very margins from which he seeks to liberate African Americans.

The Apaches operate as the mechanism to identify the common struggle now both Black and White must overcome to finalize Civilization's victory over Savagism. At a time when the nation was attempting to rectify social injustices committed against African Americans a film depicting both Whites and Blacks working in unison for the same cause supported a cohesive struggle for "freedom." The tragic result of this cinematic strategy is that the unified struggle of the two people is still the elimination of "Redskins." *Sergeant Rutledge* suggests that in learning the "metaphysics of Indian-hating," African Americans have earned their proper place in society. In a colonizer society there are two spheres of existence. *Sergeant Rutledge* suggests that it is time to let the African American into the privileged position of the colonizer. The Indian, on the other hand, must continue to exist in the home of the colonized. As representatives of the colonized world, the Indian inhabits, "a place of ill fame, peopled by men of evil repute."[22]

Lurking in both the physical and emotional darkness in the film *Sergeant Rutledge* the Indians are not of this world. The Apaches in the film are a reminder of the place where only those qualified to confront the dangers of savagism can enter. In this manner, Braxton Rutledge as savior of the White woman, Mary Beecher (Constance Tower) and rescuer of his besieged unit, has proven himself worthy of the acceptance into the civilized community. *Sergeant Rutledge* depicted John Ford's metaphoric view of the nation's struggle for equal rights. It is evident that in Ford's vision of America the Indian still has no place. As a reminder of the evil prowling the fringes of civilized society, the Indian acts as a metaphor that enlightens America to a need to include African Americans into the mainstream battle for progress.

It is during the 1960s that my particular introduction to the "Childhood Indian" first began. On television I watched Ben Cartwright and his sons occasionally battle an obstinate Paiute or merciless Apache on *Bonanza*, or perhaps, one of those Indian films from a bygone past on a Saturday afternoon television matinee. Along with my television instruction I received a steady dose of first run feature film westerns at the local theater or drive-in. Not all the westerns had Indians, but interspersed within the weekly-renewed double feature was that Indian film that reminded me, and the many children sitting alone with me in the dark confines of our visual classroom, of the dangerous and vile savage previous film eras had depicted.

Films such as *Cheyenne Autumn* (1964) led the vanguard of 1960s westerns where "guilt often mixes with sympathy."[23] Although Indians continued to appear as the hostile and dangerous savage in dozens of 1960s westerns, Hollywood was committed to a cinematic path where the depiction of Indians was meant to foster a social awareness amongst Whites. During the 1960s this social awareness still called for Indians to act as metaphor, rather than as actual Native subjects affected themselves by the Civil Rights Movement. The Indians of John Ford's *Cheyenne Autumn* act as a representation of a generically oppressed people. The Indian experiences are meant to generate recognition of society's inhumanity to itself. Film historian Jacquelyn Kilpatrick explains the incarceration of the Cheyenne in

Cheyenne Autumn, " the comparison to German concentration camps of World War II is unmistakable and obviously intentional."[24] Kilpatrick claims a Polish sergeant's comment declaring the similarity of U.S. Army Indian policies to those of his people by the Cossacks "only because they are not the same" maintained Ford's use of the Indian as a metaphor of inhumanity to society, rather than an actual victim of inhumanity.[25]

A *New York Times* film review of *Cheyenne Autumn* sums up its self-absorbed guilt complex when it described the emotional impact of the film as "a stark and eye-opening symbolization of a shameful tendency that has prevailed in our national life—the tendency to be unjust and heartless to weaker people who get in the way of manifest destiny."[26] The turmoil created by the Vietnam War further solidified the Indian as symbolic vessel of the oppressed. Ralph Nelson's *Soldier Blue* (1970) reflects Hollywood's attempt to fuse the sympathetic Indian to the anti-war rhetoric.

In *Soldier Blue* a naïve U.S cavalryman Honus Gant (Peter Strauss) and a former White Indian captive Cresta Lee (Candice Bergen) witness a series of wartime atrocities culminating in a U.S. Army attack on a peaceful Cheyenne village where the Indian inhabitants are massacred. Nelson claims he got his idea for the film, and the scene in particular, from recently exposed American military war crimes in Vietnam.[27] Nelson's depiction of the role of the lunatic Colonel Iverson (John Anderson) in the massacre of the Cheyenne suggests that his behavior and that of his men is an anomaly. According to Kilpatrick, "Cresta and Honus represent the majority, the *sane* (Kilpatrick's italics) white people who would never do such a thing."[28]

As metaphor for Vietnamese victims of crazed U.S. military fanatics, the Cheyenne reminded Americans that the Vietnam War atrocities publicized in the news were not the fault of the vast number of

159

citizens opposing the war. However, the real-life Native experience within the story is subsumed by Nelson's anti-war metaphor. Like most Indians of the 1960s, the *Soldier Blue* Indians were not meant to represent any actual Native American experience, but the idealistic imagination of Hollywood writers and directors immersed in their own version of the White (sub)Conscience. *Soldier Blue*'s release came at a time when Hollywood was re-creating its Indian into a more "realistic" character. As the 1960s came to an end, the allegorical Indian's place in American cinema also ended.

American 1960s westerns helped reinforce the conventional Indian of national mythology and sympathetic figures of the 1950s to the modern character that a new wave of children will recognize as "authentic." Americans had long ago (mis)appropriated the Native identity as theirs and called it "Indian." The post-civil rights America was much more astute and less gullible than its predecessors. Hollywood needed far more spectacular special effects to entertain its audiences. *Star Wars* (1977) technology replaced *Forbidden Plant* (1956) special effects. People wanted realism within the imagination of cinema. Similarly, the "real" Indian of the feathers, war paint and loincloth genre was replaced with a technologically more "authentic" Indian.

As both the allegorical and generic Indians vanished into history, Hollywood entered an era where society demanded a more "authentic" Indian depiction. This did not prove a problem to the ever-resilient film industry. The complex Indian of the 1950s generated a character revolution that Hollywood never fully recovered from, but modern filmmakers have made this awkward change work in their favor. Within its White (sub)Conscience experience the context of Hollywood's Indian "authenticity" fabricated an Indian-ness that now conceals the very essence of both the colonizer mentality and paternalist White Father.

In an age when Native American communities find themselves coming under harsh attacks over resources and gaming rights, the new "authentic" Indian is far more dangerous to Native self-determination than any of the previous versions of Indian representations. During the nineteenth and early-twentieth centuries Indian reformers laid out a series of plans they believed would help the Natives. Beginning with Jeffersonian America's civilizing of the noble savage to the Dawes era assimilationist schools to John Collier's Indian New Deal, benevolent legislation has resulted in cultural genocide, increased health problems, poverty and high rates of alcoholism.

White America's answer to Native American predicaments has been to find a solution rooted in Euro-American provinciality. In making movies that depict "authentic" Indians and honor Natives Hollywood merely revives the age-old tradition of doing "for" the Indian. All the Indian tropes and iconography Americans have come to recognize and love are woven into complex scripts that misguide the viewer into believing they are seeing realistic depictions of Native Americans. What they see is the "Childhood Indian" that the latest generation of young Americans will use to identify their Indian.

ENDNOTES CHAPTER 5

[1] Toby Miller, et al, *Global Hollywood*, London: British Film Institute, (2001), 41-42.

[2] Althea C. Huston, et al, *Big World Small Screen: The Role of Television in American Society*, Lincoln: University of Nebras Press, (1992), 21-23.

[3] Richard Slotkin, *Gunfighter Nation: The Myth of the Frontier in Twentieth-Century America*, Norman: University of Oklahoma Press, (1998), 347.

[4] See Slotkin's "Studies in Red and White: Cavalry, Indians, a Cold War Ideology, 1946-1954," in *Gunfighter Nation*.

[5] Slotkin, *Gunfighter Nation*, 359.

[6] See John Foran's "Discursive Subversions: Time Magazine, t CIA Overthrow of Mussadiq, and the Installation of the Shah," *Cold War Constructions: The Political Culture of United State Imperialism, 1945-1966*, edited by Christian G. Appy, Amhers University of Massachusetts Press, (2000), pp157- 182.

[7] Foran, 182.

[8] Michael Barson and Steven Heller, *Red Scared: The Commie Menace in Propaganda and Popular Culture*, San Francisco: Chronicle Books, (2001), 110.

[9] Barson, 111.

[10] "NSC 68: United States Objectives and Programs for Nation Security (April 14, 1950), *American Cold War Strategy: Interpreting NSC 68*, edited by Earnest R. May, Boston: Bedfo Books, (1993), 26.

[11] Sharing the Cold War image of menacing creature with the Indian was of course the monster. In *Seeing is Believing* Peter Biskind describes the various monster images that assisted Hollywood in warning Americans of the communist danger. From space invaders in *The Day the Earth Stood Still* (1951) and *It Came From Outerspace* (1953) or the gigantic "Red" mass devouring all that crossed its path in *The Blob* (1958), sci-fi films sustained the socio-political paranoia of the unknown and the "Red Menace."

[12] The film was later released under the name *Cavalry Charge*. Today the film is circulated for sale under the *Cavalry Charge* title, making the search for *The Last Outpost* in its commercial form a more difficult task.

[13] Walter LaFeber, *America, Russia, and the Cold War, 1945-1996*, 8th edition, New York: The McGraw-Hill Companies, Inc., (1997), 96.

[14] LaFeber, 97-98.

[15] Ray B. Brown, "Foreword," *Hollywood as Historian*, edited by Peter C. Rollins, Lexington: University of Kentucky Press, (1983), ix.

[16] Phillip French, "The Indian in the Western Movie," *The Pretend Indians: Images of the Native Americans in the Movies*, edited by Gretchen M. Bataille and Charles L. P. Silet, Ames: The Iowa State University Press, (1980), 100.

[17] Bannon will describe the Chiricahua as "...the most vicious Indian on Earth."

[18] Tom Englehardt, *The End of Victory Culture: Cold War America and the Disillusioning of a Generation*, Amherst: University of Massachusetts Press, (1995), 99.

[19] When analyzed within a Native American construct, Toriano dream called for Indigenous People's self-determination and economic self-reliance. The most essential of Native demands today, but quite subversive within an American belief system.

[20] George Kennan, "The Sources of Soviet Conduct," *Foreign Affairs*, (July 1947), 566-82.

[21] Both Fanon and Memmi write of the colonizer's perceived fears of people of color as a key component of the colonizer mentality. This danger acts as a mechanism to defend the use of violent force against people of color. For an in depth view of the development of this ideology with American literature see Dana D. Nelson's *The Word In Black and White: Reading "Race" in American Literature 1638-1867*, Oxford: Oxford University Press, (1993).

[22] Frantz Fanon, *The Wretched of the Earth*, New York: Grove Press, Inc., (1966) c1961, 32.

[23] Michael Hilger, *From Savage to Nobleman: Images of Native Americans in Film*, Lanham, Maryland: The Scarecrow Press, Inc., (1995), 177.

[24] Jacquelyn Kilpatrick, *Celluloid Indians: Native Americans and Film*, Lincoln: University Of Nebraska Press, (1999), 68.

[25] Kilpatrick, 68-69.

[26]"The New York Times Film Reviews," New York: *New York Times,* December 1964.

[27] Dan Georgakas, "They Have Not Spoken: American Indians Film," *The Pretend Indians*, edited by Gretchen M. Bataille and Charles P. Silet, Ames: The Iowa State University Press, (1980) 138.

[28] Kilpatrick, 78-79.

Chapter 6
Lord John Morgan and Lt. John Dunbar
To The Rescue:
Revisionist Hollywood and Sustaining
The
White (sub)Conscience.

During California's 2003 gubernatorial recall election, the Republican candidate Arnold Schwarzenegger employed a television ad attacking one of his rivals for having accepted Indian casino money. The ad implied that taking the money was unethical. More importantly Schwarzenegger actually accused the candidate of pandering to Indian gaming interests and implied that he would protect Californians from this kind of political chicanery. Schwarzenegger reassured the television audience that he would force Indian casinos to pay their fair share in tax revenues. The days of Indians living off the capitalist gains of hard working Californians were going to end. After his victory in November 2003, he still kept up the offensive and reiterated his accusations of Indian's unfair economic exploitation of California citizens. In November 2004 California voters voted the conscience of the governor and passed legislation placing state limits on Indian gaming income and forcing the industry to "pay its fair share" of tax revenue.

That an individual of such notoriety can use such inflammatory, and racist, accusations in the twenty first century is a testament to the resilience of America's White (sub)Conscience. Schwarzenegger dipped into the most revered of Euro-American myths to successfully campaign for office. For centuries American intellectuals, politicians, religious leaders, businessmen and plain folk have identified the Indian as a source of personal danger and threat to civilized white people. The trope was so believable that it became a staple of the earliest Hollywood westerns. Today, an era asserting the values of racial diversity, any use of divisive language targeting one particular ethnic group as a social pariah appears out of touch with the nation's values.

During the past twenty years Americans have witnessed Los Angeles Dodger General Manager Al Campanis get fired in 1987 for claiming Blacks lacked "certain necessities" to be successful in baseball management; in 1988 CBS Sports prognosticator Jimmy "The Greek" Snyder was released from his duties when he tied the success of Black athletes to mating strategies of the antebellum South; and as recently as 2003 conservative political pundit Rush Limbaugh had his contract terminated with CBS when he made racially insensitive remarks about the Philadelphia Eagles African American quarterback Donovan McNabb. Based on these high profile incidents one might be led to believe that Americans have little tolerance for people questioning the legitimacy of non-Whites rights to equal social opportunity. Yet, nary a voice was raised when Mr. Schwarzenegger accused Indians of using their federally protected gaming privileges to cheat California taxpayers of their hard earn income.

It seems that even in an age when Americans battle against the last vestiges of racism in society, they cannot distance themselves from their long standing images of Indians. Californians refused to condemn Schwarzenegger for his offensive remarks about Natives because most Californians are unaware that their belief in the age-old trope identifying the Indian as a threat to the safety of White/civilized society is anachronistic and racist. That Californians ignored Schwarzenegger's implied attack against Native Americans in an age when nationally recognized characters making ethnically offensive remarks are roasted in the press and fired from their positions, suggests a double standard towards racial intolerance or, racial intolerance to some races while growing sensitivity toward others.

This work has attempted to lay out the foundations of those ideological elements contributing to the continued attack on Native identity even as society claims otherwise. The White (sub)Conscience suggests that decades of film characterizations depicting a white/colonizer concept of Natives (recognized under the name Indian), as uncivilized savages, dependent, and subservient to whites, absolves Americans of their collective guilt for five hundred years of exploitation. Under various names and causes the exploitation still continues today. In the national consciousness the exploitation is merely a byproduct of the paternalist management of Native resources caused by their dependency on their cultural and technological superiors. This idea reassures Americans of the need to manage and protect the property Natives. Under this conviction, Native sovereignty becomes an irrelevant political indulgence. In each case, Native sovereignty is ignored in the name of progress as some government agency decides the allocation of valuable Native resources. Most of these resources will generate profits for white businesses at the expense of Native economies.

Based on these age-old axioms of Native inferiority and dependency, today's American audiences are hard pressed to believe any legislation circumventing Native sovereignty is unfair and morally inappropriate. Despite what the national party line suggests, civil rights, multiculturalism and diversity does not include Native Peoples. Contemporary Hollywood portrayals of Indians continue to suggest the same culturally backward, technologically inept, dependent savage. All that has changed is that Indians are depicted in more anthropologically accurate ways. However, this successful marketing tool does nothing more than create one more layer of the national self-denial associated with the White (sub)Conscience.

Part of the success of the White (sub)Conscience lies in the ability of mainstream America to create a

167

visual imagery of Indian-ness that fits the national conscience. As explained in chapter two, Americans have used Indian imagery within a social or political construct as symbols of contemporary discourses. Indian-ness became the property of American discourse and has taken various shapes over the course of the nation's history. Sometimes the Indian was depicted as a character of Nature imbued with all the qualities a colonizer society used to deny its exploitative nature. Anti-Native racist attitudes were justified by the savage, uncivilized and deceitful characteristics of these natural Indians. At other times, the image became a metaphor for contemporary political or social movements. In either case, in a real life context the Native was relegated to the socio-political and economic margins. Under various literary or cinematic guises Americans were reminded of the marginal social value "Indian-ness" has to offer contemporary society.

In 1950, Delmer Daves' *Broken Arrow* began a trend in American film making that makes it even more difficult for Natives to rid themselves of the demeaning and inaccurate assumptions American society holds so dearly to its bosom. But, it is the cinematic "innovations" of the past three decades that have truly embedded into national consciousness false depictions of Indians that allow Americans to continue their collective attack on Native sovereignty and culture. In 1970 *A Man Called Horse* ushered in the era of the "authentic" Indian; Native Americans have yet to recover from this Hollywood "innovation." Upon its release I found myself duped by its suggested depiction of Indians.

It was in 1970 that I was first introduced to the Torres', a Mescalero Apache family, and the matriarchal woman who died in 2002, and to respect old customs, whose name I will not use, but whom I was instructed to addressed as "Grandmother." On the few occasions when I was invited to lunch or dinner Grandmother made us sandwiches, a meatloaf, or spaghetti. Once in a

168

while I'd be treated to a bowl of chili with a fried bread that was very similar to the "buñuelos" my own grandmother made during Christmas. There were references to "*gahes*" and "*bik egudi ndé*" and White Painted Woman,[1] but their very "American" behavior never suggested any "Indian-ness."

As the Torres family was opening their doors to me at one level, my mainstream upbringing continued to obfuscate reality. Back home in California, I found myself mesmerized by the schoolyard discussions about *A Man Called Horse* and its depiction of "real" Indian life. Friends kept on saying, "If you want to see what it was like to be an Indian, see *A Man Called Horse*." The movie itself received a testimonial from the Smithsonian Institution's own chief "ethnohistorian" Wilcomb Washburn, who claimed *A Man Called Horse*, was "The most authentic description of American Indian life ever filmed."[2] When I saw the film in the theater I was terrified by the frightening customs of these people. What kind of people forced an old woman to die like an animal of starvation because her son had died? I was most dismayed however, at the male rites of passage that required the insertion of bones into the chest and then being lifted into the sky to dangle until one ripped the bones from the chest. All I could say was, "I'm glad I'm not a Sioux boy."

The Sioux mistreatment of their captive Lord John Morgan (Richard Harris) was a reminder of the dangers one faced in the American frontier, replayed over and over in many westerns from early film generations. Ironically, this "authentic" state-of-the-art film reinforced a childhood of Hollywood films depicting Indians as warmongering fiends ready to strike out at innocent White people. Little did I understand that what director Elliot Silverstein considered "authentic" in *A Man Called Horse*, many critics considered a cultural abomination. According to film scholar Raymond William Stedman, the most glaring

169

violation of Native cultural representation in the film was the use of Mandan ceremonies being conducted by the Sioux tribe.[24] A box office success, *A Man Called Horse*, along with the equally successful revisionist western *Little Big Man* (1970), set off a Hollywood strategy that depicted "real" Indians in its westerns. Indian authenticity became obligatory to the narrative. What followed during the next three decades was a plethora of westerns depicting anthropologically more accurate Indians. The narratives however, maintained the same cultural biases against Natives that filmmakers have been using since D. W. Griffith produced *The Battle of Elderbush Gulch* (1914).

In addition to *A Man Called* Horse, and *Soldier Blue*, *Little Big Man* (1970), was the third of the "Holy Trinity" of westerns that helped transition Hollywood's depiction of Natives Americans from the generic Indian to the more "authentic" Indian that contemporary viewers now come to know as the "real" Indian. However, even as this film is lauded for its depiction of the old Native wise man Old Lodge Skins (Chief Dan George), it incorporates American cultural stereotypes and standards to depict other critical aspects of the film. Native American homosexuality is used as comic relief, depicting the characters as off-Broadway drag queens in buckskin, never considering the cultural context homosexuality may play in Cheyenne society. The homosexual characters were mere caricatures of an Anglo-American homophobic stereotype. Adding to *Little Big Man*'s significant flaws is the depiction of the Indian killer George Armstrong Custer as a deranged lunatic, once again portraying the white Indian killers as psychopaths living outside the norms of traditional American beliefs. The film representation of a deranged Custer sooths the guilty conscience of a White (sub)Conscience America. Even within a script's alleged accurate depiction of Natives the Hollywood

170

story has time to defend the values of society's colonizer roots.

In the decades to follow it became appropriate for filmmakers to depict their Indians as visually authentic as possible. Although the genre took a considerable hit at the box office during the 1970s and '80s, a few "B" westerns such as *Winterhawk* (1976) and *Grayeagle* (1977), with White actor Alex Cord playing the title role, maintained allusion of the authentic Indian. What audiences observed as accurately dressed Indian characters compensated for poor, listless scripts. Hardly Oscar quality, these films generated a nostalgic and romanticized image of Indians that no doubt helped increase the sales of portraits Noble Red Men and Indian Country scenery at swap meets and flea markets. However, by no means does this work suggest that the colonizer mentality Indian was forced to the Happy Hunting Ground.

Hollywood did not give up its savage and menacing Indian without a fight. While the transition to the more "accurate" and sensitive portrayal of Indians was finding a foothold in the national conscience, the cinematic tradition of villainous Indians did not die without a fight. During the 1970s films such as *Chato's Land* (1972), *Ulzana's Raid* (1972) and *Against a Crooked Sky* (1975) kept the dependable murderous Indian image on the silver screen. In Michael Winner's *Chato's Land*, Chato (Charles Bronson) a half-breed Apache with blue eyes systematically kills the members of a vigilante gang that raped his wife and killed his kin in a series of acts that are more appropriate to a horror film. Robert Aldrich's *Ulzana's Raid* depicts a U.S. cavalry unit's chase of a marauding Apache war party. All the traditional Indian characteristics are addressed in the film: from rape to torture to fatalistic Indian spirituality. *Against A Crooked Sky* was much the same. A December 1975 *Variety* review described it as a film that "Harks back to the not-so-good old days when

Indians were depicted as lascivious villains bent on kidnapping white girls and murdering pet dogs.... It's amazing that the film was made in 1975."[3]

In general, throughout the mid-1970s and early 1980s, the western suffered at the box office. By the mid-1980s, the noticeably Indian-less, western box office hit *Silverado* (1985), suggested the acceptability of the genre back into the mainstream. The film most associated with the actual revival and, more importantly, the promotion of the authentic Indian to a new generation of viewers was Kevin Costner's western abomination *Dances With Wolves* (1990). Like Delmer Daves *Broken Arrow*, *Dances With Wolves* was considered an innovative film that portrayed Natives in ways unlike any previous work of its kind. While the use of Native American actors and the use of Lakota dialect in the script are commendable features in an industry notorious for its insensitive portrayals and hiring record of people of color, lurking in the screenplay are the sinister qualities associated with the White (sub)Conscience.

It is a mistake to describe *Dances With Wolves* as anything less than the defining western of its generation. Since its 1990 release and subsequent rampage on the Oscars, critics and the general public have come to recognize *Dances With Wolves* as the most accurate depiction of Indian life. Kevin Costner has become the Indian authority of his generation. The movie itself has been proclaimed for its "politically correct statement."[4] However, despite its supposedly innovative portrayal of Indians, *Dances With Wolves* is nothing more than one more influential White man displaying a fantasy shaped by his White (sub)Conscience and Turneresque or even, Joseph Conrad-like, view of history.[5]

From the moment Costner's character, Lieutenant John Dunbar, sets foot on Nebraska soil at his post, Fort Sedgwick, the viewer is bombarded by a series of classic western tropes that are done with such artistic pageantry that apparent homage to Indians is subtly overwhelmed by the most fundamental features of the White (sub)Conscience. Beginning with *Broken Arrow* any good Indian film required key elements to appear, as not to confuse the viewer. These features are rooted in the very literary tropes Americans have maintained about Natives for centuries. Without these cues viewers will be confused and thus not fully enjoy the pretext.

If there is one important factor viewers have learned from good Indian films it is that where there is a good Indian there must be a bad Indian. Costner had been inspired to depict the epic story of the Great Plains' most famous occupants, the Lakota, or Sioux. The Lakota are portrayed as peace loving, humorous and caring; they mourn the loss of friends; enjoy yarns of heroic hunting exploits; break bones and worry when food is scarce. However, Hollywood Indian formulas necessitate the depiction of mean-spirited, coarse and downright evil Indians too. Costner will follow this proven recipe and give the audience his Pawnee.

The man who the *Internet Movie Data Base* (IMDB) identifies as, "The Toughest Pawnee" (Wes Studi) leads Costner's Pawnee. As explained in chapter two, a critical component of the colonizer mentality is the generalization of Native attributes. No character better embodies the "quintessence of evil" that Fanon claims colonizers ascribe to Natives than the nameless Pawnee. In his brief appearances, the nameless Pawnee will mock his hunting party's concerns over a White's campfire; he will murder, mutilate, and scalp a lonely teamster; kill the parents of the White heroine twenty years earlier; lead a raid on the defenseless Lakota village; slam a tomahawk in the back of the village elder (a number of times); and challenge his executioners with a blood-curdling war whoop just before they fire in unison at the human beast. The nameless Pawnee's behavior is a reminder to the audience that the frontier was a dangerous place for the weak of heart, where fierce nameless Natives were all too ready and willing to strike at the innocent.

The second critical component of the good Indian cinematic strategy was the eventual salvation of the Natives by the benevolent White hero. In *Dances With Wolves* Lt. Dunbar will commit no less than four gracious acts of assistance for the Lakota; acts that no doubt were critical to the tribe's survival. After he has made acquaintances with the Lakota, Dunbar races into the village during a ceremony and while the ungrateful Natives pummel him for probably disturbing a religious ritual, he explains that he has discovered the whereabouts of a herd of buffalo. The starving Indians have been desperately seeking the buffalo and were oblivious to their location. Apparently, the thunderous hoof clapping of the large herd that had awakened Dunbar fell on deaf ears in the nearby village.

During the hunt, which Dunbar is invited to participate in, he saves a young Lakota boy named Smiles a Lot (Nathan Lee Chasing His Horse) from a rampaging bull with a miraculous shot from afar while sitting on his horse. The bull is downed only a few feet from the stunned boy who in his fear forgot to try and run from, or attempt to dodge, the animal. Later in the film, when the bulk of the Lakota men are on a war campaign against the Pawnee, the very same Pawnee have sent their own war party against the Lakota village. Against U.S. Army regulations Dunbar uncovers a cache of Government Issue rifles, and distributes them to the Lakota warriors remaining in the village so they can defeat the invading horde. Unlike *A Man Called Horse*'s infamous scene where Morgan forms the Indians, also Lakota, into English bowmen's ranks to fend off the enemy's attack, Dunbar merely provides the weapons. His Indians are not as martial arts impaired as Morgan's Sioux. Dunbar's final benevolent act is leaving his adopted Lakota family to remove them from the danger of an American force he knows will track him down. Ever the paternalistic benefactor, Dunbar takes his White woman into the winter cold to protect a people he obviously believes are no match for the American military.

There is absolutely nothing revisionist about Costner's *Dances With Wolves*. It is an unabashed defender of White Supremacist doctrine. Although obfuscated by a pretense of cultural recognition and homage, *Dances With Wolves* sustains the timeless elements of a colonizer society in the guise of entertainment. Costner, both as actor and director, succeeds in depicting the comfortable images of Indian/White relations Anglo Americans want to see. Bad Indians are hideous creatures warranting extermination and the good Indians exist due to the benevolent nature of the paternalist White hero. In either case, Whites relate to the inferiority of Native culture, even as they are awed by its "authentic" quaintness. Friends would discuss the beautiful scenery in the film for days, or marvel at Lakota's ability to pick up their belongings and move on a moment's notice, or even how sad it must have been to be an Indian when your entire world is being destroyed by the encroaching Whites; but they will never discuss the inferiority of Indians to the technologically more advanced American society. This is a point the White (sub)Conscience allows Americans to savor internally; it is never openly acknowledged, it is only accepted.

After Dunbar/ Dances With Wolves helped the Lakota villagers defeat their Pawnee assailant his voice over described his feeling of power over having participated in a battle where there were no "dark political objectives," but "fought to preserve the foodstores that would see us through the winter," and then revels in the sound of his Lakota name being called over and over. This event is a moment of triumph, not for the Lakota, or even the Lakota wannabe, it is for the colonizer that still lives in all Americans. As cultural anthropologist Nicholas Thomas posits,

> Dunbar's nominal indigenization is also a moment of conquest in two senses. Not only does he help defeat the Pawnee, but he establishes himself as a champion among the Sioux, who recognize the power of the weapons he has introduced and make him the hero of the moment, calling his name over and over. This interpellation does not identify Dunbar as a Sioux, and is not what his self-discovery consists in. Instead, his prior self-recognition as a soldier in battle possessing 'dark' political significance is transmuted into his recognition by the Sioux as a heroic warrior; he never becomes a common member of their community, but retains the privilege of the colonizer to act forcefully and with historical effect....[6]

Costner has made the question of race a critical component of his narrative, whether he intended to or not. One other significant feature in *Dances With Wolves* not yet addressed in this work, but a vital element in the racist rhetoric of the White (sub)Conscience, is the question of miscegenation.

For the better part of the history of cinema, the union between White and Indian characters was strictly taboo. During the good Indian period ushered in by *Broken Arrow*, films such as *Broken Arrow* (1950), *Across the Wide Missouri* (1950), *The Savage* (1953), *Jeremiah Johnson* (1972) and *A Man Called Horse* (1970) address the problematic union between a White man and Indian woman by conveniently killing off the Native heroine. In those films where the two live on, they will remain with the Indian woman's tribe, or go off to live by themselves in the wilderness. Civilized America has no room for interracial marriages.

Somehow in an era that our society claims is more tolerant of race, Costner plays the interracial cinema question in a manner that is an insult to a multicultural society, yet is done so brilliantly, that it goes unnoticed. In creating a love interest for Dunbar in a place where civilized Whites are a distant thought, in a society devoid of racist fears of miscegenation, the soldier will merely find the most beautiful girl in the camp and marry her, of course, according to Lakota law. Simple, yes, but for some unknown reason Costner is uncomfortable with portraying an interracial romance between Dunbar and a Lakota woman. Instead he introduces a captured White woman, Stands With A Fist (Mary McDonnell), who has lived with the Lakota for so long she barely remembers her English. Stands With A Fist dresses like a Lakota and speaks their language. Other than a hairstyle that appears to have its origins in a 1980s rock concert, she is as Indian as the Lakota women, although this Stands With A Fist does have the genetic potential to reintegrate into white society.

By creating a culturally indigenous woman who is actually White; who incidentally is thrust into her cultural cross-dressing position by murderous Indians, (none other than the nameless Pawnee), Costner circumvents the highly offensive White Supremacist question of race mixing, while passing himself off as a pluralistic and culturally sensitive moviemaker. When the hero and Stands With A Fist ride off into the Colorado winter, Costner conforms to an American ideology both conservative and liberal figures claim no longer exists in this society.

Dances With Wolves has such a highly charged White (sub)Conscience mystique to it that even when critics denounce it, their reasons are founded on principles of stereotypical Indian-ness that harkens back to a simple time when complex Native images didn't confuse the viewer as to the "real" nature of the Indian. Western historian Wayne Michael Sarf's 1991 critique of *Dances With Wolves*, titled "Oscar Eaten by Wolves," is replete with criticisms of the film that are very

177

reminiscent of Richard Schickel's 1975 elegy to single-dimension cinematic Indian dripping in the blood of White victims, "Why Indians Can't Be Villains Any More." Sarf's complaints about the film center on technical issues that he feels fail to depict the Lakota as an imperialistic, warmongering, gang-raping society that valued the art of torture and mutilation of corpses.[24] Although Sarf is correct in identifying the Lakota as recent arrivals to the Great Plains, he fails to explain the complex series of events, which was actually set in place by European contact, which drove the Lakota into the territories they occupied when they first interacted with the United States government.[7]

Sarf's harsh attack on *Dances With Wolves* is a glaring example of the persistence of the White (sub)Conscience even within the academic world. In his article Sarf accuses historian Dee Brown, author of *Bury My Heart At Wounded Knee* (1970), of abandoning "history for the more lucrative field of propaganda."[8] He defends the bulk of his arguments with anecdotal stories depicting Native atrocities against Whites. He considers *Dances With Wolves* a modern-day revisionist good Indian film, a genre he believes Americans have little need for, yet he never condemns the openly racist anti-Indian westerns Americans have also been exposed to. Without acknowledging his own subliminal ideology, Sarf's inconsistent critique of *Dances With Wolves* translates into an acceptance of the racialized imagery of Natives that Americans are accustomed to reading about or viewing on a screen. This repulsive academic work is indicative of the kind of a White (sub)Conscience American mindset. As an example of the scholarly condemnation of the film, in contrast, those in Hollywood who support Costner's successful Indian film formula will inundate the 1990s with "feel good" Indian films that do nothing more than extend the basic principles of a paternalistic ideology during a time when Native sovereignty finds itself under renewed attack.

Hollywood actually found itself reviving the romanticized Indians of late-nineteenth century literature condemning Indians to a "vanishing" experience. Cinematic Indians lived in the past, not the here and now, a bygone time that progress and modern American technology have long since left behind. Thus, American cinema can produce a litany of Indian films weakening arguments supporting Native rights to an entirely new generation of "childhood" viewers.

With this philosophical foundation, little wonder Hollywood would produce an abundance of films holding true to the basic principles of modern-day cinematic Indian-ness. A byproduct of *A Man Called Horse* and subsequently proven a cultural and financial mainstay by *Dances With Wolves,* Hollywood's Indian will be as "authentic" as script writers can imagine them. Rather than representing Native communities with respectful and culturally sensitive portrayals, cinematic representations are caricatures of a bygone era and an archaic racist past. Yet the image thrives. In a culturally sensitive America, Hollywood screenwriters will share their White (sub)Conscience ideology with a cross-section of social characters.

Thus, the seemingly benign White presence in a film's narrative takes on the much more significant role of juxtaposing dependent Indian culture against the morally, intellectually, and physically superior White society, therefore justifying capitalist-driven exploitation of Native resources. The inaccurate Indian images young boys and girls viewed on television forty years ago became their historical references for contemporary Natives. Their children have been introduced to the same stereotypical Indian their parents grew up with, but with a more creative pretense that is indicative of the seemingly more culturally astute viewer. Each story depicts "authentic" Indians in the most ludicrous of situations, yet the "childhood Indian" influence of the earlier eras is reinforced by a modern "childhood Indian"

179

generation that guarantees the believability of the pretext.

During the 1991 baseball playoffs, Ted Turner, owner of the Atlanta Braves, came under pressure from Native groups for fan's use of the "tomahawk chop" and war whoops.[9] The following year, Turner's Turner Network Television (TNT) began producing a series of made for television pro-Indian films that appear to have been created to counter those complaints against his baseball team's fans. One of these films was the 1992 made for television Christmas special, *Miracle in the Wilderness*, in which Dora Adams (Kim Cattrall) tells her Blackfeet captors the story of the birth of the baby Jesus. As the dumbfounded Blackfeet listen to Dora's narrative of her people's Christmas tale, the cinematic story cleverly incorporates a Native American presence. In an obvious attempt to make Christmas a Native inclusive event, the characters in the story Adams tells her Blackfeet captors are portrayed as Indians. An Indian Mary and Joseph struggling to find a place for her to give birth to her child venture to a Great Plains Sun Dance where all the tribes will attend: including Sioux, Cheyenne, and Cherokee.[10] During the gathering Indian Mary gives birth to baby Indian Jesus and are soon joined by the three wise men, "Teton," "Mandan" and "Plains Cree," who came to worship the baby.

Throughout the film, like the *1001 Arabian Nights* heroine, Scheherezade, Dora and her husband Jericho Adams (Kris Kristofferson) fend off death by mystifying the child-like Blackfeet with their storytelling ability and superior intelligence. At one point Adams' narrative is interrupted by the mid-winter birth of a fawn, and ever the sagacious couple even as prisoners, the Adams's calmly explain to the incredulous and evidently wilderness deficient Indians that the birth is a Christmas miracle. In an earlier scene, the cabin-living Adams family stoically stands against strong storm winds as the buffalo-skin teepee-dwelling Blackfeet cower against nature's forceful presence. The contrasting images of the Adams's standing firm against the harsh winter wind and the Indians cringing against nature's forces is a metaphoric reminder of the superiority whites maintain over Natives, even in a Native's own environment. A post-Colonialist interpretation of the two incidents just described requires only a minimal of Fanon and Memmi to identify the white supremacist context. The existence of white supremacist metaphor in a 1992 film supports anti-colonialist theorist Thomas Gladwin's argument that defending concepts of racial superiority is paramount to maintaining the psychological white supremacy.[11] Convincing whites of the racial superiority of whites is as important as reminding the non-whites to their racial inferiority to whites. Even in an film depicting an indigenous Christ birth the makers of *Miracle in the Wilderness* must include the most rudimentary of colonizer logic.

Despite the Indian Mary and Joseph presence, the film is replete with the White supremacist references necessary to sooth the conscience of a colonizer society, rather than a multicultural or diverse society. A climactic hand-to-hand fight between Jericho and the Blackfoot warrior, Many Horses (Sheldon Peters Wolfchild) defines one more element of the colonizer mentality Americans claim no longer exists (some may even argue, never did exist!). Needless to say, Jericho defeats his Indian foe, but, like a good White man, spares Many Horses' life. Many Horses is reformed and in gratitude releases his benefactor from captivity. In the context of the good Indian film, would Many Horses have been as generous to Jericho had he gained the upper hand over his White foe?

Equally as ridiculous is another pair of made for television films, *Black Fox* (1995) and its sequel, *Black Fox: The Price of Peace* (1995). Both films are set in post-Civil War Texas and, like John Ford's *Sergeant*

Rutledge three decades earlier, attempts to incorporate Blacks into the mainstream narrative of westward expansion. In an era of multiculturalism, these films depict a Black man in the role of the traditional great white hero. While the casting of a Black man in the hero role is commendable, the portrayal of the Kiowa Indians resuscitates the archaic savage construct, while employing Hollywood's artistic licensing tenet to create "realistic" Indian customs that violate the principles of "authenticity" *A Man Called Horse* introduced in 1970, and *Dances With Wolves* confirmed in 1990.

In the first movie, after some Kiowa steal horses from frontier families, Britt Johnson (Tony Todd) rides off to return the horses from the Kiowa, while his "brother," and former master, Alan Johnson (Christopher Reeve) seeks to keep anxious white settlers from starting a frontier war. Although Alan Johnson must confront danger from fellow white neighbors eager to kill the Kiowa, the "multicultural," "honorary white" Britt Johnson, faces the Indian horde only white heroes were permitted to challenge in earlier westerns. The sequel maintains a similar story, except this time the prize is not horses, but a white woman, a battered white woman. Britt Johnson saves the same Kiowa in the first film from a white man seeking to start a war against the tribe in order to recapture his abused wife. To prove that Indians are just as capable as whites of committing domestic spousal abuse, Britt will also save a Native woman from her wife-beating husband. Insulted by the loss of his woman to the outsider, the Kiowa husband, who had kidnapped the white woman, challenges Johnson to the "traditional" Kiowa duel of tug-o-war over a rattlesnake pit. In a multicultural twist on the "Man Who Knows Indians," Johnson, the African American, out-Indians the Indian and defeats the abusive man. The war between the two people is averted due to the fortuitous intervention of the non-Indian, a Black man imbued with the virtues of white America.

Along the same multicultural motif, Charles Haid directed *Buffalo Soldiers* (1997), his homage to African Americans in the military. According to Internet Movie Data Base (IMDB) film critic Jack Sacksteder, "the film examines the racial tension between black soldiers and some of the white soldiers and the truth about the Indian invaders."[12] As a forum for examining race in the military during the late-nineteenth century the film probably merits viewing consideration, however, it has a typically implausible Hollywood ending.

Referencing their own experiences with the contemptible institution of slavery the Black troopers refuse to obey an order to attack the sleeping encampment of Victorio's Chihenne Apache. In a decision reminiscent of the Vietnam era Black Power anti-war slogan, "No Viet Cong ever called me a Nigger!" the cavalrymen refuse to fire on a people they empathize with, leaving the slaughter of the Apaches to White soldiers, or as history will actually record the massacre of Victorio and his Chihenne to Mexican forces, under the command of General Joaquín Terrazas. In this case, the more humane people were the African American Buffalo Soldiers; in today's multiculturally sensitive America, Haid can let Blacks play benevolent White master to the powerless and dependent Indian.

During the 1990s Hollywood also produced pro-Indian films that continued to include these misrepresented images of Natives. In *Black Robe* (1991) the Iroquois were depicted as misogynistic goons devoid of any compassion, while the Huron guides to the French priest are portrayed as more docile and manageable. *Last of the Mohicans* (1992) follows the script of the 1936 version,[13] thus audiences were assured of an evil-incarnate Indian, Magua (Wes Studi), and a scene where colonists were brutally murdered by Indians. Walter Hill's excruciatingly painful *Geronimo: An American Legend* has the Chiricahua leader sparing the life of an American miner who refused to back down from his

Apache captors. Impressed by the miner's valor Geronimo orders all the other miners killed, sparing only the man who challenged his Indian enemies. Disney's feature film cartoon *Pocahontas* (1994) gave America an environmentalist who would have made *Playboy* proud. The following year *Last of the Dogmen* (1995) has Professor Lillian Diane Sloan (Barbara Hershey) and Lewis Gates (Tom Berenger) discovering a Cheyenne village in hiding since the 1864 Sand Creek massacre. Gates risks his life to find penicillin for the injured son of the chief. The two White social misfits gain acceptance in the tribe and the couple are allowed to live in paradise with their Indian friends. Director Frank Oz has a little boy, Omri (Hal Scardino) bring a toy Iroquois warrior to life in *The Indian in the Cupboard* (1995). The pint-size warrior, Little Bear (Litefoot) becomes Omri's mentor, and although the young boy will learn many valuable lessons from Little Bear, the visual relationship between the gigantic looking child and diminutive mature Indian sustains a strong subliminal colonizer manifestation of Natives. During the multicultural 1990s heroic White figures continued to overshadow the Indian heroes.

Although the films examined in this chapter are but a small cross section of the generous helping of Native American themed motion pictures, these examples display the common denominator in Hollywood's portrayal of Indians. No matter how much the industry claims to want to present the Native American in a multi-dimensional, culturally sensitive image, society's internalized ghosts are difficult to exorcise. The vestiges of colonialism's paternalistic, White supremacist narrative continue to influence the role of White characters in many of these films in relationship with Natives. Whether we are willing to admit to this, as Peter Biskind has clearly pointed out, films are a reflection of society's beliefs. During the recent wave of revisionist Indian films, the message remains the same as it has been since Hollywood began making westerns: White supremacy, and Indian inferiority and dependency. With this theme clearly imbedded into the mind of American viewers, as children and later adults, there is little doubt in the mind of the public that while Indian-gaming is one way of relieving the nation of its communal guilt over its treatment of Indians, the Native is still a ward of the government and in desperate need of American supervision.

Based on the images presented on film, it is obvious although Native American society has a nostalgic, idyllic, and sometimes tragic quality to it, it cannot stand up to the onslaught of American civilization and Progress. This kind of logic leaves Americans believing that only when Natives have successfully assimilated into mainstream society can they be entrusted with determining their own future. But who decides when the Native is assimilated? The Five Civilized Tribes assimilated many Jeffersonian era virtues just before they were forcibly removed from their Southeastern homelands to Indian Territory during the 1820s and 1830s.

Contemporary Hollywood westerns have given the impression they are presenting a truly innovative Indian image, when in fact they are continuing to express the age-old colonialist themes of White supremacy, Paternalism and Native dependency. In turn, mainstream America internalizes these "new" concepts as the most accurate depiction of present-day Natives. The harm in this portrayal is that Whites continue to identify Native Americans in a nineteenth century vacuum, thus refusing to think that any contemporary issues could affect Native people. Assured through film that Native Americans are culturally backward and dependent on American society's aid, the public confidently leaves it up to government agencies to manage the economic affairs of Indian people. History has shown that government agencies established for overseeing the welfare of Native Americans, institutions influenced by paternalistic notions that White reformers know what is best for the Indian, leave a scene of cultural and social destruction in their wake.

A form of Dunning School "Negro incapacity" suggests that Natives are incapable of governing themselves without the assistance of white benefactors.[14] With this in mind, rather than an intrusive measure denying Natives self-determination, government control of Indian affairs acts as a cleansing agent, washing the hands of the American public clean of any wrongdoing related to private industry's government-sanctioned expropriation of Native resources. During the very same period Hollywood has reminded America of its compassion for Indians over the course of two, beginning a third, childhood Indian generations, corporate America and the governments of the United States and Canada have used their paternalistic benevolent counsel to subject Natives to a colonizer exploitation as rapacious as any colonial empire that history has condemned.[15] North America's government agencies charged with the protection of Native Americans and their resources, the U.S. Interior Department's Bureau of Indian Affairs (BIA) and Canada's Department of Indian and Northern Affairs (DIAND) are working in confederation with private enterprise to utilize Native resources at the expense of indigenous welfare.

Through the use of veiled, and sometimes blatant, colonizer propaganda in Indian themed films during the past half century Hollywood has convinced the public of Native dependency upon White society, and of the necessity for American paternalistic guidance. On at least one occasion, this paternalistic guidance has resulted in the second largest radioactive spill in the United States affecting the Navajo Reservation at United Nuclear Corporation's uranium mill in Church Rock,

New Mexico on July 16, 1979. Over 100 million gallons of contaminated water was released into the Rio Puerco when a millpond burst. The heavily contaminated water affected over 1,700 Diné and their livestock, and while the public raged over the nuclear disaster at Three Mile Island in March of the same year, the Native calamity was condemned to anonymity. Balking to acknowledge any responsibility for the accident, United Nuclear Corporation refused to provide the Native residents with adequate emergency water and supplies.[16] A government report claiming the Diné had suffered "little or no damage" as a result of the spill absolved United Nuclear Corporation of any blame.[17] The company agreed to an out-of-court settlement and paid $525,000 to the victims.[18]

According to American historian/activist Ward Churchill, during the late-1970s, forty energy corporations targeted the second largest concentration of Natives in North America for uranium mining, including the "Sioux Complex" that encompasses large areas in North and South Dakota, the Shoshone and Arapaho people of Wind River Reservation, and the Powder River Crow and Northern Cheyenne.[19] A similar incident to the Church Rock contamination occurred near the Pine Ridge Reservation in 1962, and by 1980 the Indian Health Services declared the well water for the nearby village of Slim Buttes had radiation three times the national safety standard. A new well tested at fourteen times the level.[20] After considerable government procrastination the Slim Buttes problem was resolved by removing the uranium tailings to an exposed plateau a few miles closer to the reservation, secured by a chain link fence and barbed wire, and a "Hazardous Waste" sign warning.[21]

Likewise, Canada's First Nations are not immune to the government's expropriation of Native lands in the name of progress. Athapascan, Cree, Inuit, and Anishinabe in Canada's northern territories are victims of hydroelectric development plans. Although the Cree communities were awarded a total of $135 million and Inuit received $90 million, the James Bay watershed was forever negatively altered. When completed in 1984, the James Bay project cost over $20 billion; three times what the Canadian government originally predicted.[22] Canadian citizens' protest was confined to cost overrun. Because the government was providing an essential commodity (electricity) for urban America (U.S. Northeast corridor) and the consensus Canadian view was that its leaders knew what was best for its indigenous charges, nary a voice was raised to challenge the adverse affect the project had on Native society.

In 2005 Congress passed the Energy Policy of 2005 (HR6), allowing for exploration for petroleum in Alaska's Arctic National Wildlife Refuge (ANWR). Controversy has risen over the effect drilling will have on the wildlife, including the 130,000 strong Porcupine (River) caribou herd. For over ten thousand years these animals have provided the local Native community the Gwich'in, with the primary source of their protein diet. Recent fears over rising gas prices has given President Bush and the Republican-controlled Congress a mandate to find petroleum sources, even at the expense of the cultural integrity of Native communities.

Hollywood's misrepresentation of Indians facilitates the continued exploitation of Native resources and ignores the negative impact on indigenous communities. Despite its seemingly altruistic deeds, Hollywood's portrayal of Natives in its films serves to perpetuate the repugnant and immoral ideology denigrating the very people the cinematic industry claim to honor. As Biskind argues, films are only a reflection of society's values; Hollywood gives the public what it wants to see.

While Anglo-American society is more than willing to accept good Indians in westerns, the narrative is more palatable if the hero is a White man. Hollywood's Indians continue to depict the Frederick Jackson Turner Indian, the savage as an obstacle to the progress of civilization. Although today's cinematic Indian is seen more sympathetically than Turner or Theodore Roosevelt could imagine in their wildest nightmares, the message is nonetheless as clear today as it was a hundred years ago, or a century before that. The savage Native can only survive under the firm, but well meaning, hand of the white master.

The virulent colonial discourse of an earlier generation of American oppressors has morphed into a righteous, egalitarian seeking crusade for the historically oppressed and marginalized who suffered at the hands of people from an era less humane than today's "culturally sensitive" America. Today's society has only succeeded in raising the standard of self-delusion. Although the Civil Rights movement has opened many doors for women and people of color, the fundamental tenet influencing America's support of equal rights circulates back to the age-old colonizer belief that the white race knows what is best for the Native people of this world. Equal rights in today's America require a commitment to concepts delineating capitalistic (white) cultural superiority. Within this racial construct, American society measures equality, diversity, and multi-culturalism in terms of how well marginalized communities have accepted the mainstream (white) worldview, including contemporary views on race issues. Just as whites justified their economic and spiritual defilement of Native communities by declaring the latter culturally, morally, and intellectually inferior people, today's white dominant class vindicates its usurped ruling status by feeding the masses the artificial concept of equality, while maintaining deep seated fears of the loss of cultural, economic and social hegemony to Natives.

The same fears that motivated white colonizers to create overtly oppressive institutions is inducing the current society, dominated by the White (sub)Conscience to develop less overt, yet, equally exploitative strategies. The questions of Native American sovereignty or Indian self-determination are moot points so long as the American society retains its stranglehold on the White (sub)Conscience inspired image of Natives.

Ever since Hollywood discovered the marketability of the cinematic Indian during the 1910s, thousands of American films have made their way on to the silver screen or television. Some films history will recognize as epics, box office smashes, critical milestones or simply B-movie wretchedness, best shipped off to oblivion. Regardless of the success these films had during their first run, most continue to live on television. With the proliferation of satellite television and hundred plus channel capabilities, the exposure of these films to viewers is boundless. This work has not only sought to explore the power of cinema to influence the minds of its viewers, but more importantly to expose the subliminal ideology this nation has developed over the course of its existence to defend exploitative actions against people of color, most specifically Native peoples.

The primary force motivating this project is this nation's delusional belief in an America open to all peoples, where people are chosen on "merit" rather than the color of their skin. This nation was founded on racist principles. For the better part of its history one might say it reveled in its racist, segregated (one can even argue misogynistic) society. The law of the land protected the rights of White America to exploit and abuse to its capitalistic content, whether the person wore a white robe standing behind a burning cross or a black robe sitting in front of an American flag, both de facto and de jure sustained the basic principles of a colonizer society.

The ideas generated from this concept are too soothing to the ear and soul, and cleansing to the spirit of White America. The childhood identity problem, resolved as an adult, is directly related to a maturation influenced by the power of the visual medium. Although social movements continue to sway the minds of humankind, those actions continue to face the formidable myth of White, cultural and physical, supremacy. As Australian cultural anthropologist Nicholas Thomas argues racism manifests itself within a society as it "emerges from a particular tradition and vocabularies through which human difference is recognized."[23] Regardless of successful civil rights legislation, or claims to political correctness and cultural diversity, these issues are all filtered through the conscience of a society indoctrinated to the innate inferiority of the Brown "other." Literature, film and television are not the cause of the oppression of people of color. They only provide the mechanism for the propaganda.

However, this study does not intend to cast accusations towards one particular segment of American society. This is a transgression all Americans must accept culpability for; the flaw exists in the way most Americans see the "other." Today's volatile global climate is a lesson for Americans who firmly believe that all people of color hold an irrational hatred towards the United States. The White (sub)Conscience continues to justify U.S. political, economic, and military aggression against those nations refusing to submit to "compassionate" American leadership. The Indians have changed, but the target is still the same. Today's object is a people of color possessing different customs and values from those of Americans, and coincidentally, they are possessors of vast quantities of resources vital to maintaining American's high standard of living.

It is our way of thinking that must change. It is an old way of thinking that has been harmful and malicious. The films and television programming incorporating Indians, or other people of color, will continue to exhibit the same insensitivity to Native culture that American literature described early in the nation's history. The vivid color and narrative brought to life through the visual medium is too powerful a tool for the viewer to discount, no matter how inaccurate or malicious the story may be. Small treasures, such as *Smoke Signals* (2000), *Doe Boy* (2001) and *Skins (2002)* do not have the viewership to sway enough Americans from the womb-like security the White (sub)Conscience provides its believers, with its paternalistic portrayal of Native Americans.[26]

In each phase of the Hollywood Indian image, the one constant of White superiority defined the social place of the Native in American society. In their pre-World War II identity Native peoples characterized evil incarnate, the most fundamental of American literary Indian iconography. During the post-World War II "good Indian" period, Natives offered Hollywood the opportunity to demonstrate how benevolent white men could be when pressed to rescue the less fortunate. Within the context of the Cold War, the Civil Rights Movement and the Vietnam War, the Indian played the consummate metaphor of the social and political needs of the time. Most recently, when revisionist Hollywood came calling, the dignified Indian became the symbol of a bygone era of American history, yet still gave screenwriters the latitude to include the subliminal white supremacist ideology. Though no longer acceptable overtly to this generation of viewers, it remained still very much a part of their national ideology. The White (sub)Conscience has allowed Americans to rationalize the delicate issues of racial and social inequalities without endangering the racist beliefs fueling the nation's capitalist expansion.

192

The renowned American historian Robert Berkhofer, Jr. once claimed that the greatest paradox of United States Indian policy is the "heritage of its failure and success." Attempting to stamp out Indian-ness with a humanitarian approach, while seeking to dispossess Natives of their lands and resources led to conflicting results. Berkhofer explains the paradox: "If the United States government had spent more money and effort in ruthless suppression of tribal cultures and expropriation of tribal resources, the Indian problem would indeed have disappeared." He continues, "Thus humanitarian sentiment prevented the suppression of Indian life at the same time that economic individualism drastically reduced Native Americans' resources to support such separateness without further aid from White government."[27] Native sovereignty is undermined because the United States government, Corporate America and American society fail to see within their myopic social view the inconsistency between their desire for Native lands and resources, and their yearning to cleanse their conscience of any wrongdoing.

Obfuscated by the rhetoric of America's multicultural and diversity cant is the reality that the racist principles this country was founded on and thrived on for nearly two centuries have endured within the ideological construct of the White (sub)Conscience. Race scholar John L. Hodge argues the importance of the dualism of good and evil in a racist, colonizer society as "a necessary part of the justification of oppression."[28] Hodge continues,

> Without dualism, there would be no perceived conflict or contradiction.... It would be a compliment to say Blacks sing and dance. It would be a compliment to say women are in touch with their emotions and feelings. But to the extent dualism exists, these compliments become insults. The images are intended to insult, and they *do*

(Hodge italics) insult to the extent that dualism is *assumed* (Author's italics). [29]

The White (sub)Conscience sustains the very essence of this behavior, and Hollywood has succeeded in defining the dualistic nature of Indian/white encounters. According to Hodge, dualism suggests it "reasonable to reward with more power and rights those who are seen closer to good; similarly, it is reasonable to restrict the power and rights of those seen as less good."[30] During the past half century Hollywood has employed this dualistic strategy to depict the Indians that it claims it is honoring. Thus, cinema acts to strengthen the racist ideology of an America not yet ready to allow Natives the rightful place mainstream America claims Native Americans deserve.

Forged from the very ideology it publicly condemns, the United States uses popular culture to divert attention from its colonizer abuse of Native Americans. None are more successful contributors to this practice than Hollywood. As a multicultural America enters the twenty-first century, television viewers are guaranteed an endless supply of westerns that will both entertain and remind them of the socio-political place Native Americans hold in our perceived world and maintain in the real world. The result of Hollywood's role in sustaining the White (sub)Conscience is that another generation of Natives will battle for political and economic self-determination with the support of those Americans influenced by the Childhood Indians of a bygone cinematic genre. Inculcated by a cross-section of Indian images misrepresenting Native culture at the most egregious levels, those childhood Indian viewers are now influencing a new generation of gullible Americans. This wave of sophisticated viewer will *know* the "real" Indians according to contemporary Hollywood Indian conceptualization.

194

In 2003, former child star Ron Howard released his homage to the West, *The Missing*. In a 2004 interview for the Starz Network promoting the film, Howard claimed he wished to represent the West as he perceived it. The storyline of my childhood Indian contemporary's film has the daughter of a man's estranged daughter kidnapped by a hideous looking Apache medicine man who appears more a Cro-Magnon than a nineteenth century Native. The medicine man's evil incarnate character is countered by the White hero gone Native (portrayed by Tommy Lee Jones, who by the way, speaks better Apache than the Native actors playing Apaches), who gallantly sacrifices his life to kill the medicine man and save his family's lives. In an era influenced by "diversity" and "multiculturalism," that has allegedly long since distanced itself from the blatantly racist ideology of a bygone age, the works of "innovative" directors such as Howard remind us that the White (sub)Conscience thrives even in the best intentioned and brilliant minds.

ENDNOTES CHAPTER 6

[1] In the Chiricahua and Mescalero cosmology, *Gahe* are the mountain gods important in protecting the People from dangerous spirits; they are most commonly seen during the Maidens' puberty ceremonial, but they also bless homes and other important community events. *Bik egudi ndé* literally translates into "The Giver of Life." White Painted Woman is the most revered character in Apache cosmology; her connection to fertility and the continuation of life make her especially important during the Maidens" puberty ceremonial.

[2] Ward Churchill, *Fantasies of the Master Race: Literature, Cinema and the Colonization of American Indians*, San Francisco: City Lights Books, (1998), 173.

[3] Raymond William Stedman, *Shadows of the Indian: Stereotypes in American Culture*, Norman: University of Oklahoma Press, (1982), 222.

[4] Michael Hilger *From Savage to Nobleman: Images of Native Americans in Film*, Lanham, Md.: The Scarecrow Press, Inc., (1995), 191.

[5] Wayne Michael Sarf, "Oscar Eaten by Wolves," *Film Comment* XXVII/6, Nov-Dec 91, 62.

[6] See Conrad Ostwalt, "*Dances With Wolves*: An American *Heart of Darkness*," *Literature-Film Quarterly* v24, n2 (April, 1996), 209-216. Ostwalt sees *Dances With Wolves* as author Michael Blake's American examination into colonialism and self-discovery, comparing the work to Joseph Conrad's classic critique of late-nineteenth century English adventures in Africa.

[7] Nicholas Thomas, *Colonialism's Culture: Anthropology, Travel and Government*, Princeton: Princeton University Press, (1994), 181.

[8] An unabashed Custerphile, his AOL address is "custerfact," Sarf had a history of works that either defend traditional views of history or criticize deviation from this ideology. In his warped scholarly interpretation denouncing his hero's chief Native rivals, the Lakota, somehow makes Custer appear more a heroic figure. His two works *The Little Big Horn Campaign: March-September1876 (Great Campaigns)*, Scranton, Pennsylvania: Perseus Books Groups, (1993) and *God Bless You, Buffalo Bill: A Layman's Guide to History and the Western Film*, New York: Fairleigh Dickinson University Press, (1983) are prime examples of his longing for the Parkman, Bancroft, and Turner influence of Western history.

[9] See Richard White's "The Winning of the West: The Expansion of the Western Sioux in the Eighteenth and Nineteenth Centuries," *Journal of American History*, September 1978, 319-343, for a well-balanced and provocative look at Lakota migration. White argues that pressure from the Cree and Assiniboine combined with economic and social needs influenced Lakota migration on to the Great Plains. Focused as he was on highlighting Lakota atrocities Sarf failed to mention, as White does, that the arrival of European traders during the late-eighteenth century proved significant in the Lakota's westward expansion.

[10] Sarf, 64.

[11] Jacquelyn Kilpatrick, *Celluliod Indians: Native Americans and Film*, Lincoln: University of Nebraska Press, (1999), 121.

197

[12] As ridiculous as it sounds, Dora Adams does place the Cherokee of the American Southeast in a Great Plains ritual.

[13] Thomas Gladwin and Ahmad Saidin, *Slaves of the White Myth: The Psychology of Neocolonialism*, Atlantic Highlands, N.J.: Humanities Press, (1980), 48-49.

[14] HTTP://us.imdb.com/plot?0118790. From an academic perspective Mr. Sacksteder's review is as problematic as the film. The quotation in the body of this work gives a hint of this problem, "...truth about the Indian invaders?" Sacksteder refers to Vitorrio (Victorio) and his Apaches as invaders of Mexico and New Mexico. Had Victorio been leading Ojibwe or Haudenosaunee his argument would be quite valid, but to call Ndé invaders of their own homeland, it is a downright historical crime.

[15] Hilger, 241.

[16] See Eric Foner's critically acclaimed, *Reconstruction: America's Unfinished Revolution, 1863-1877*, New York: Harper & Row, Publishers, (1988), for an informative criticism of the old Dunning School's racist interpretation of Reconstruction, and the school's insistence on "Negro incapacity," or the Black community's socio-political incompetence, as a reason for the use of harsh measures to control the South's Black community.

[17] None greater an example of the disastrous effects of colonialism than the Columbus-era genocidal malfeasance towards Caribbean Natives, or the French treatment of the Vietnamese during the great famine of the 1930s when over one million Natives died of starvation while French granaries remained copiously secured shut. Although the current results of corporate

abuse has not reached the genocidal proportions of the two examples, the long-term results of many of the capitalist projects targeting Native lands have the lasting potential to undermine Native American sovereignty, while contaminating, or altering, Native homelands to the point of destroying the life sustaining capacity of the region.

[18] Marjane Ambler, *Breaking the Iron Bonds: Indian Control of Energy Development*, Lawrence: University of Kansas Press, (1990), 175.

[19] "EID Finds Church Rock Dam Break had little or No Effect on Residents," *Nuclear Fuel*, March 14, 1983.

[20] Frank Pitman, "Navajo-UNC Settle Tailings Spill Lawsuit," *Nuclear Fuel*, April 22, 1985.

[21] Ward Churchill, *Struggle for the Land: Indigenous Resistance to Genocide, Ecocide and Expropriation in Contemporary North America*, Monroe, Maine: Common Courage Press, (1993), 276-278.

[22] "Radiation: Dangerous to Pine Ridge Women," *Akwesasne Notes*, Vol. 12, No. 1, Spring 1980, 1.

[23] Churchill, *Struggle for the Land*, 280.

[24] Churchill, *Struggle for the Land*, 341.

[25] Thomas, 14.

[26] It is no coincidence that these three cinematic gems depicting Native Americans in multi-dimensional and contemporary roles have Native American directors; Chris Eyre for *Smoke Signals* and *Skins*, and Randy Redroad for *Doe Boy*. This evidence is a testament to contemporary Hollywood's inability to look at Natives

beyond the images it has inherited from generations of White filmmakers. Amongst Native American's associated with Hollywood there is a strong sentiment that the only way Natives will be portrayed honestly is by getting Indian people to produce their own films. They may be right.

[27] Robert Berkhofer, Jr., *The White Mans' Indian: Images of the American Indian from Columbus to the Present*, New York: Vintage Books, (1978), 193.

[28] John L. Hodge, "Equality: Beyond Dualism and Oppression," *Anatomy of Racism* edited by David Theo Goldberg, Minneapolis: University of Minnesota Press, (1990), 96.

[29] Hodge, 97.

[30] Ibid.

Epilogue:
Revisiting Boonesborough,
the Quest for Adventure, and Misplaced Thoughts.

During the months that I began touching up this manuscript I decided to mix in some baby-sitting duties for my two children with the editing. In between playtime and naps my three-year old and I would sit down in the workout room and watch some of "pápas" nostalgic DVD collections. As I've had a chance to think about some of my entertainment selections I am reminded of how difficult it is to break old habits and the power childhood memories have in determining our wistful viewing pleasures; and more importantly for me, the dangers of falling victim of my own theory. Although intellectually aware of the racial context of programs I shared with my little boy I still find myself drawn to many of those television shows I know are replete with White (sub)Conscience elements and strongly racialized issues. I hope that as time passes and I watch these programs with my son while he matures and develops a better comprehension of what his father is trying to teach him, he will understand that separating intellectual and entertainment perceptions of cinema and television does allow us to view programming we may find offensive from a race context.

If I were to eliminate from my viewing every film or television program imbued with White (sub)Conscience subtexts I'd never turn on a television again (Actually a blessing!). Over the course of my research, and countless viewings, and re-viewings, of racially insensitive material, I have learned to separate my theoretical perception of a program from its entertainment value. This work is inspired by the belief that if exposed to principles of the White (sub)Conscience viewers can recognize the harmful portrayals of indigenous people on the screen is not representative the true contemporary existence of these people. Over the past century, many of the films depicting indigenous people might be considered classics, some even national treasures. Most, however, are little more than ninety minute program filler. My intention is not to suggest a boycott of every film depicting Native Americans unfavorably, but, instead to make audiences conscious of themes of Indian/White relations they are being exposed to in the film in a White (sub)Conscience context. As intelligent, socially-conscious viewers aware of the flawed cinematic race imagery they are viewing, we may still enjoy the artistic context of the products from a bygone era, with the hope of nonetheless being able to affect future film-making decisions. Therefore, I owe it to my son to reflect on some of the television selections his father has made for their viewing pleasure.

A favorite playground for my son was the family workout room where a television monitor allowed for the playing of programs while working off a few pounds. Children's toys made their way into the room and slowly transformed the landscape into a bizarre combination of athletic equipment, blocks, and toy trains. Wednesday morning television time became a ritual for the two of us, my little boy would begin to play and I'd pop in a DVD from my "old school" collection, and regardless of what my son, Daniel, was doing, immediately upon hearing the theme song to the television series *Daniel Boone*[1] he'd stop turn around and sit down. He would attentively listen to the theme song watch a few minutes of the program and then get back to the more important task of playing with his toys. Nonetheless, his response to the *Daniel Boone* theme song is a testament to the catchiness of the tune and its place as an American pop culture icon. Fess Parker developed the character and series in 1964 after Walt Disney refused to let Parker use his Davey Crockett character in a Parker production. Stuck on a frontier theme, Parker settled on a program using the frontier hero, Daniel Boone. *Daniel Boone* never replicated the Crockett phenomenon of the mid-1950s, but during its six-year run the series developed a loyal audience, and like many historical-based fictional series or films, left viewers believing there was some element of truth to the stories, despite the Hollywood "artistic licensing" factor very prominent in these productions.

In my case, I am drawn closer to the series today for a number of reasons, one being Parker's attempts to make the series relevant to an audience embroiled in the tumultuous late-'60s Civil Rights and Vietnam debate without alienating his viewers. While Parker stayed away from Vietnam themes, civil rights elements did make their way into many *Boone* scripts. When Fess Parker died on March 18, 2010 I wrote my own personal eulogy to him on my Facebook page. In it, I pointed out that despite *Daniel Boone*'s historical inaccuracies I held Fess Parker in deep respect for his idealistic approach to race relations, yet the *Daniel Boone* series still embodied many of the paternalistic, virtuous, and benign elements of the White (sub)Conscience demeaning and insulting to Native Americans.

Parker displayed a genuine respect for indigenous people; however, from a White (sub)Conscience perspective his characterizations are anything but respectful. No 1960s series better employed the "generic" Indian like Parker. It was almost impossible to distinguish between Cherokee, Tuscarora, Shawnee, Creek or any other Indian that ventured near Boonesborough: although Mohawks did have their iconic "Mohawk" hairstyle to identify them more easily. "Generic" Indians aside, few Indian deaths occurred during the six seasons; even really bad Indians were more likely to be converted by the end of the episode. These were not the bloodthirsty savages of the American Indian trope. These Indians were much more tolerant of Americans and open to discussion and negotiation, but like the "Good" Indians of 1950s cinema, it was the White man, in this case, Boone, teaching Indians the value of peaceful coexistence. The flawed Native American depictions in *Boone* were endless. Yet it is his trusted Indian companion, Mingo (Ed Ames), whose role proves problematic.

A regular during the first four seasons, Boone's faithful companion the mixed-blood Cherokee Indian, Mingo, educated at Oxford through his wealthy English father's connections proved the antithesis to the naïve Indian reoccurring throughout the series. Time after time the educated Mingo put ignorant frontier settlers in their place with his intelligent and eloquent dialogue. At the height of the Civil Rights Movement Mingo was the small screen foil to those Americans still struggling with the concept of educated and equal persons of color. Yet, in quintessential White (sub)Conscience logic, Mingo's respectability came from his English education; there were not a few occasions when the Oxford-educated Indian had to fight his Indian-ness to prevent his "savage" side from getting the better of him. Mingo proved that, given the proper education, dark-skinned people were just as functional as White Americans, but that equality came from his ability to conquer his innately inferior Indian way of life and adopting the sometimes flawed, yet morally and culturally superior dominant culture. In *Daniel Boone* being an Indian was not a sign of progress.

When Ed Ames left *Daniel Boone* to reestablish his singing career, Parker took his time replacing Mingo. During season five Gabe Cooper (Rosey Grier) ventured in and out of the series until he became a full-fledged member of the *Boone* family in season six. Gabe Cooper gave Parker a double-barreled civil rights icon, Grier, a former professional football player and high-profile African-American activist, portrayed an escaped slave who became a Tuscarora chief. Dressed in traditional "generic" Indian garb Gabe Cooper represented a very common early-American occurrence.[2]

It is true that many escaped slaves did seek sanctuary amongst Native communities, most married into the tribe and became productive members. This time, *Boone* had the Tuscarora choose Gabe as their chief, from a White (sub)Conscience perspective it is obvious that the Tuscarora were impressed with Cooper's enormous size[3] and couldn't help making him their leader. Parker installed a civil rights era Black man as the leader of an Indian tribe.

As in John Ford's *Sergeant Rutledge*, Black America was welcomed into a previously White exclusive club. The *Rutledge* African Americans had the opportunity to fight and kill the menacing savage; in the case of *Daniel Boone*, Cooper became the paternalistic father figure. While the *Rutledge* Blacks exterminated the heathen, Gabe Cooper rescued the Indians, just like Audie Murphy, Dale Robertson, James Stewart and numerous others did during the "Good" Indian era of the 1950s. Parker merely replicated the standard perception of child-like Indians easily drawn to a stronger, more superior figure; in this case, his civil rights conscience transferred the privilege of ruling over Indians to a Black man.

Daniel Boone's White (sub)Conscience breaches are representative of an individual whose well-intentioned heart conflicted with the social perception of Indians he had grown up with. A season six episode "Readin', Ritin', and Revolt" (March 12, 1970) provides an amusing side to Parker's attempt to keep his show relevant and letting his social conscious dictate scripts. When an Indian boy, Little Hawk (Tony Davis) is sent by his father, Chief Tekwatana, to Boonesborough to learn the ways of the White man the young Indian will convince his White friends of the need to also learn the ways of the Indian. When the teacher refuses to include an "Indian Studies" component to his curriculum the young boys employ the strategies Chicano, Black, and Native American students were using to force universities to implement Ethnic Studies programs to their schools.

Thirty years after the fact, the storyline is hilarious. Watching the young boys try every protest tactic the real students had used in their battles for academic equality is somewhat contrived, yet it did show pathos to Native culture; but it is hard to take seriously a movement led by another of the "generic" Indians of the non-existent "Hollywood" Indian tribe. "Readin', Ritin', and Revolt" reveals the social conscience of a man who sought to understand the turbulent times his program existed in. While never to be seen on any critic's "greatest television" episode, in paying homage to young men and women he had no contact with, "Readin'..." will stand as Fess Parker's misguided White (sub)Conscience approach to depicting indigenous themes: dependent, ingenuous, backward; Native characters depicted from a White perspective...but, he sure did try.

During the mid-2000s *Daniel Boone* returned to syndication on the Christian-based television network World Harvest Television (WHT). Even though I possessed the DVD collection, I'd still catch myself waiting to watch an episode from time to time, what came to my attention however, was a disclaimer preceding each episode declaring the following as "Educational Programming." I tried to understand in what context *Daniel Boone* could be considered "educational," it was ridiculously historically inaccurate,[4] and Indians and Blacks, in general, have a paternalistic imagery to themselves.

While there are strong moral issues that may generate "Christian" qualities, the "educational" context of *Boone* was difficult to justify; more importantly, a new generation of viewers was introduced to archaic Indian images...with a Christian television stamp of "educational" approval. Unwittingly WHT endorsed the negative portrayal of Indians, thus ensuring the generational inheritance of the demeaning and paternalistic images of indigenous peoples at a time when American society is making claims to cultural diversity, while also demanding something be done to stem the tide of "illegal aliens." The social dichotomy this society currently displays gains momentum when innocuous negative portrayal of people of color are validated not merely through the scheduling of these programs, but more importantly, claims of "educational" value of obviously offensive racial imagery. WHTs actions is another unfortunate example of the White (sub)Conscience's persistence and the difficulty in eliminating its harmful effects. Without being critical of race, *Daniel Boone* is a program depicting the moral principles a Christian community places a premium on, and believe are "educational;" however, race is relevant, regardless how much people delude themselves from this reality.

Focused as I was on analyzing cinema, I overlooked the hundreds of cartoons my baby-boomer generation watched Saturday mornings and after school. I never put much credence in the ten minute featurettes, regardless of the stereotyping characters that made their presence every so often. I had a chance to rethink my position while watching episodes of the Hanna Barbera adventure cartoon series *Jonny Quest* (1964) with my son. I've always considered *Jonny Quest* one of my favorite Sixties series. When first released its intriguing stories, action sequences, and exotic backdrops made it cutting edge entertainment. The precocious Jonny and his Hindu companion Hadji[5] travelled the world with Jonny's father, Benton Quest, a scientist with high-level U.S. security clearance, under the protective eye of government agent, Roger "Race" Bannon, the scene was set for adventure.

An episode did not pass by that some bad guy didn't try to commit some heinous act against the Quest party. The 26 episodes provide its audience with an almost limitless supply of adventures forcing the Quests to use their superior intelligence, quick-thinking skills, and physical prowess to escape the clutches of this installments unfortunate bad guy. Not quite obvious until I had the opportunity to view the series as an adult, but *Jonny Quest*, conceived at the height of the Cold War and the growing news of wars of liberation, Mau Maus, Viet Congs, and angry dark-skinned people reflected the ever-present American fear of a Communist/indigenous alliance threatening to destroy Western society. Not surprisingly, the people threatening the Quests were either of Eastern European extraction or people of color, including the reoccurring evil genius, Dr. Zin; of some unknown Asian origin.

Included in the *Quest* adventure experience were three episodes of particular interest bringing the Quest party into direct danger at the hands of indigenous people; "Pursuit of the Po-Ho," (Oct. 9, 1964) "Treasure of the Temple," (October 23, 1964) and "A Small Matter of Pygmies" (December 11, 1964). Each of the episodes gave viewers a sample of the behavior of the "savage" still living in remote areas of the world: and they were "savages." In "Pursuit of the Po-Ho" a tribe of South American headhunters kidnapped a scientist friend of Benton Quest, when the Quests come to rescue the man Dr. Quest himself is taken prisoner. During the course of the adventure the Quest party expressed language evoking the racist dialogue of an earlier generation.

Before landing their private jet in the Amazon jungle Dr. Quest uses an amplifier speaker to call out to the Po-Ho, the family pet Bandit then gains possession of the microphone and barks loudly down into the jungle, scaring animals and Natives alike, Hadji belatedly grabs the dog and apologies to Dr. Quest for the pet's behavior. Quest responds, "The barks probably shook up those savages a lot more than I did." When Dr. Quest is taken by the Natives, Bannon angrily snaps "Po-Ho devils!" During the rescue preparation the boys ask Race what his thoughts were; to which he responds, "Those savages are building up to something." In his challenge to the Po-Ho, as the water god Aqizio, Bannon warns "...and you savages better lay off, or I'll take your village apart; stick by stick." Interestingly enough, after displaying a masterful dexterity for spear-throwing during a "test of bravery" of the captives, as in the westerns of old, during the climactic rescue scene, these Indians reverted to the classic martially deficient marksmen American audiences have become accustomed to seeing from Indians in combat, thus allowing the heroes to make their escape.

A few episodes later the Quest venture to Central America, at the invitation of an unnamed government, to investigate the discovery of an ancient Mayan city in "Treasure of the Temple." In this story the bad guy is actually a British fortune-seeker (Perkins) who has bullied local Natives to search the site for treasure. Assisting Perkins is a mestizo guide (Montoya) who leads the Quest through a series of failed ambushes before finally abandoning them to join his master. When Jonny accidently discovers the ancient treasure Perkins has been searching for to no avail, the bad guy orders his Indians to capture the Quest party, as can be expected, the two Quest men will physically manhandle the more numerous Natives, only after Perkins fires a round from his pistol over the heads of Quest and Bannon are the heroes subdued. When a Native the Quests had earlier rescued from death returns the favor to his White benefactors Quest and Bannon will overpower Perkins and his Indian stooges. The "good guys" will once again defeat the forces of evil.

The third of these problematic stories is "A Small Matter of Pygmies." In this story, Race and the boys crash-land in an unidentified jungle inhabited by "Indians." After rescuing another Native sentenced to death by his people the party is captured by those same Natives: Pygmies. Again, a grateful Indian will risk his life to rescue his White emancipators. After making their escape from the Pygmy village, Race and the boys will fend off the attackers with what appear as an endless supply of boulders and logs from their mountaintop stronghold. Each time the Pygmies gain a military advantage Race is quick to the task and neutralizes their dilemma with his ingenuity until help arrives. A White man and two small boys proved too much for these "savage."

Quest proves that it isn't always necessary to portray Indians as bad guys to maintain the White (sub)Conscience subtext. In "Turu: The Terrible" (December 24, 1964) Natives appear as helpless, child-like creatures tormented by a prehistoric animal who is managed by a deranged man using the Natives to mine a special and valuable ore. After the Quests defeat the beast the frightened Indians bewilderedly wait for the two White men to show themselves and tell the Natives that it is safe, and they are free to leave. This episode reeks of the paternalistic "Great White Father" and the colonizer mentality principle arguing the fortuitous arrival of Whites to rescue defenseless Indians from their oppressor: in this case another White man.

On a lighter side, "Werewolf of the Timberland" (January 7, 1965) generates a more humorous White (sub)Conscience perception. In this case, the mysterious Indian of the Canadian wilderness, White Feather, (always appearing with his arms crossed and speaking in a monosyllabic tone) rescues the boys from gold smugglers. In all his best "Noble Savage" accoutrements White Feather presents the audience with another of the revered Indian images from America's past. Sometimes it is just too safe to venture away from the symbols and beliefs we have been nurtured with since childhood. William Hanna and Joseph Barbera, cartoonists born during the first two decades of the 20th Century, and beginning their careers as animators during the late-1930s and 1940s, grew up with the stereotypes of Indians already criticized in this work, the two men's stories reflect the comfort of the culture they were raised in; they knew Natives only from what American culture had taught them.

In *Jonny* Quest, time after time, the language and scenes children will watch for years to come during Saturday morning network programming, during the 1990s in the Cartoon Network line-up, and as of late on the Cartoon Network nostalgia spin-off, Boomerang, will denigrate Po-Hos, Central American Indians, and Pygmies whose "savage" cultures prevent them from fully appreciating the progressive nature of a civilized (White?) world. The ideology of the White (sub)Conscience lives on in the benign images of nostalgic animation viewable to anyone with cable or satellite service.

Throughout all these nostalgia "epiphanies" I also find myself trying to apply a White (sub)Conscience context to events taking place on a national level. Trying to place the theory into a mainstream experience, Native American imagery aside; how do principles of the White (sub)Conscience project into the mainstream *Weltanschauung* of ourselves. From immigration rights marches, presidential elections, congressmen shouting out during a presidential address, even Tea Party movements are all tainted by a mind-set of racial superiority and the most primitive and instinctive elements of a colonizer mentality that identifies people of color as a physical threat to one's being. A quote used earlier from David Theo Goldberg, "Individuals may well come and go; it seems that philosophy travels nowhere" resonates in the aftermath of public rationalization denying or, more harmful, ignoring the racialized context in our actions.

When millions of Americans marched during the spring of 2006 for immigration reform these people were expressing their political voice through their First Amendment rights to freedoms of speech and peaceful assembly. Engaged in political activities many Americans have declared paramount to the very essence of the liberties and freedoms the founding fathers endowed this nation with, individuals called for their government to redress an issue they felt important enough to protest with over one million other people. However, in the months that followed polls showed that many Americans were angered by the protest. Media sources claimed there was a mainstream "backlash" to the protest for immigration reform.

Of course, if pressed to explain their position, none of the people polled would ever recognize their view as racist or anti-people of color. Yet in their arguments condemning the marchers it became evident that the sight of so many Brown-skinned protesters touched an emotional hot button manifesting itself into an angered response to the people making a political statement. That anger felt by so many Americans against the immigration rights protesters, like so many of our contemporary immigration debates, had nothing to do with racial sentiments. The issue of racism is irrelevant to the poll question; our society no longer recognizes race as a "legitimately" discussed issue. It is only a theme extremist dwell on; mainstream America has moved on and no longer considers the issue worthy of intellectual debate.

Within this ideological milieu it becomes important to reconsider the standard arguments defending immigration restrictions and the militant position on border enforcement. Most guardians of immigration restriction will apply economic arguments to their view, eliminating the need to raise the race issue. By looking into this country's immigration history the pattern of racial hostility long since held towards Native Americans enters into the equation at the end of the 19th Century, as does the argument for immigrant restriction due to economic concerns. For nearly one hundred years this country practiced a policy of open immigration, although occasion flare-ups of anti-German or anti-Irish sentiments did exist, few Americans supported a policy restricting immigration.[6]

The arrival of a people culturally and racially different than most Americans significantly altered this sentiment. Anti-Chinese sentiment in the West, manifested itself into a series of violent nativist attacks on Chinese communities during the 1870s, contributing to the first federal law to identify a specific immigrant group for immigration restriction. The Chinese Exclusion Act (1882) placed a ten-year moratorium on all Chinese laborer immigration, the plan was so popular that the Geary Act (1892) extended it an additional ten years and was made permanent in 1902.[7] Ironically, on October 28, 1886, only four years removed from the first federal anti-immigrant legislation, Americans dedicated the Statue of Liberty, a testament to this country's immigrant past, and more importantly its commitment to a principle of immigration rights. Emma Lazarus's "Give me your tired, your poor, your huddled masses..." takes on a hypocritical, hollow meaning in the shadow of the Chinese Exclusion Act.

In the decades to follow immigration restrictions were expanded to include Europe and later Latin America. In each case, increased limitations were rationalized away as necessary to protect American society. Contemporary nativist resort to this same theme of safeguarding the economy and the standard of living, or in light of 9/11, security reasons, to support immigration restrictions, militarization of the border, para-military anti-immigrant organizations and all of the fear-mongering associated with "illegal aliens." What I consider a "Chicken or Egg" question regarding the connection between immigration and economic concerns gains a prominent place in my view of this issue. Is it only a coincidence that this country recognizes the dangers of immigration on the economy when the immigrant stops coming exclusively from Northern

Europe? During the very era when immigration restrictions began the United States initiated its overseas imperialist strategy. If the nation was sending its navy and merchants to far-off shores to intimidate and force U.S. hegemonic control over under-developed countries for the purpose of expanding American markets to energize a stagnant U.S. economy, how can one justify the denial of economic sanctuary for those people sacrificing economic and social security in order to experience the growth in America's wealth and increased standard of living?

Many of the immigrants coming to the United States during the past half-century have done so due to economic and political duress resulting from corrupt governments pandering to U.S. business interests. That many of these immigrants come from countries with largely indigenous populations does not ease the crisis, nor alter the question. Is the increased concern over "illegal immigration" an economic, or race issue? The White (sub)Conscience prevents Americans from honestly performing a conscience-testing assessment of this question. Does the presence of a subculture of American (Hemispheric) citizens living in the United States without government sanctioned documents really threaten the "American Way of Life?" Biased studies on both sides of the argument will present "concrete" evidence to support their position; yes or no. Is a society claiming itself as the "Melting Pot" of immigrants, with a population hovering over 300 million, really fear that a few million "illegals" have the will or capability to subvert the social, political, and economic core of a nation who, for better or worse, have themselves altered the social intercourse of much of today's world?

That many of these immigrants come from largely indigenous populations forces one to re-examine early-America literature, the virulently anti-Indian language, and the origins of racist American ideologue; an ideological perception that will dominate American intellectual and religious dialogue well into the mid-twentieth century. When compared to the fear-driven images of eighteenth and nineteenth century Indians, the xenophobic dangers "illegal aliens" pose to contemporary American, not much has changed in the perception of the Indian; the only difference is today people are not required to admit these feelings are racially motivated.

The White (sub)Conscience obfuscates the repulsive elements percolating in the underbelly of American society, the divisive cant spewing from individuals and groups lacking the foresight to recognize the untapped wealth of cultures and societies born long before Europeans crawled out of their caves and organized their first villages prevents this nation from exploiting the abounding knowledge accumulated during the past 10,000 years as sole inhabitants of the Western Hemisphere. When analyzed without the pretense of "homeland security" or economic recessions, the colonizer mentality rationalization Americans have long denied has in reality made up the foundation of this nation's expansionist doctrine pre-dating Manifest Destiny.

As every anti-colonialist scholar, going back to Frantz Fanon, has argued, paramount to the colonizer logic of aggression is the threat, nearly always non-existent, Natives pose to the former's health. During the last half-century indigenous "illegal aliens" have endowed the nativist Americans with the metaphoric Indian who will, like the misrepresented image of old, endanger society; the exploitation, hate-mongering and fears of the unusual and foreign thrive. Placed in its proper context, anti-immigrant as Indian metaphor is but a minor piece in the larger understanding of how the White (sub)Conscience fits into today's America.

Many a time in class I've lamented to my students that the Civil Rights Movement, has in large respect, been a failure. Now, I try to point out to them

215

that, yes, there have been great strides taken during the past fifty years for people of color, but, using a grading context the students could relate to that explains its theoretical failure, understanding the movement's shortcomings becomes more visible. I argue, when graded on a 100 point scale the movement only scores a 59, a point short of a D, and 11 points short of passing. The movement did score some big social points, but it failed to answer far too many key issues to warrant a passing grade: including, eliminating the influence of race within our national conscience. Almost immediately after passage of the landmark Civil Rights Act (1964) critics of the movement began to use language and arguments attacking the government's financial commitment to Civil Rights, and with the tension and political maelstrom that was the Vietnam War, support from liberal Whites began to wane: the backbone of political support for the movement. The "angry white male" political strategist turned analyst Kevin Phillips identified in 1968 who helped Richard Nixon win election was emblematic of the changing tide against civil rights ideology. By the time Nixon was elected President with the goal of taking America back to the "happy days," a time, obviously, before the radical voices of Civil Rights disrupted the normalcy of the 1950s, much of the nation was ready to move on without Civil Rights. Thus, without even leaving the 1960s the preliminary grading out of Civil Rights as already grim, but more failings are to come.

Other than my graduation in 1977, the Seventies was fairly uneventful, and could have been skipped; *M.A.S.H.*, John Denver, Disco, Grape Nuts, Son of Sam I think we could have spent our time more wisely. Civil Rights received something of a reprieve, but the 1980s brought us Ronald Reagan and his Cold War crusade to prevent the "...destruction not only of this Republic, but of civilization itself."[8] The remnants of Civil Rights were offered up for sacrifice to the altar of "containment" in the name of George Kennan and Paul Nitze. While defense spending increased dramatically under Reagan, social programs, education, environmental protection, the arts all experienced severe budget cuts.

As Civil Rights experienced a slow, lingering death, "Dutch" made political appointments assuaging the conscience of those fearing he lacked sympathy for people of color; selections that reeked of tokenism, carefully selected Women, Blacks, and Hispanics received prominent individual political posts, but in the larger context these communities watched their economic and political energy drained throughout the decade. I've strongly felt that it was during the Reagan era that the White (sub)Conscience entered into the national consciousness. Cloaked under the earthy, grandfather-like, leadership of Ronald Reagan Americans were happy to leave behind any moral obligations to racial and gender equality an earlier generation naively committed its children to complete.

The conscience was cleansed and the country moved on; diversity, multi-culturalism, and political correctness entered into the national vernacular. No one could accuse this country of racism, only extremist still considered the ideology significant in today's America. This kind of logic is the key ingredient in formulating a White (sub)Conscience state of mind. What follows during the Nineties will be the acquittal of four LAPD officers in largely White, middle-class, Simi Valley for the beating of a "career" criminal Black man, yet race did not influence the jury. A stunned...no, angry White America will listen as a jury acquits O.J. Simpson for the murder of his wife and her friend. Were they angry because the legal system failed to convict a man who the evidence proved was guilty? Or, were they upset because a wealthy Black man learned to play the system that for years was the exclusive domain of affluent White men?

The racial context to the response of the verdict by Whites flew under the radar; pundits, women's groups, late-night television criticized or mocked the acquittal but stayed away from the race question, although they did accuse Simpson's lawyer, Johnnie Cochran of using the "race card" during the trial. Vilified for introducing race to the case, Cochran exemplified the "desperate" misuse of race to win an argument; but in a society convinced it has eliminated racial inequalities, when does race matter?

Even more debilitating to exposing the nation's failure to recognize sustained racial biases in its behavior will be the 2008 presidential election. Barack (Barry) Obama was elected 44th President of the United States; if this nation can elect a Black man president, isn't that proof enough that this country is truly "color-blind," and beyond reproach for its racial beliefs? To the contrary, the election of Obama epitomizes everything that is wrong with the White (sub)Conscience.

As this society has moved past the Civil Rights Movement, seen Blacks, Mexicans, women in more responsible and respectful positions; as housing, employment, education and interracial marriage restrictions have been eliminated, it has become accustomed to the sight of these formerly marginalized Americans performing everyday activities; "heck, they can even move in next door to us....if." It is true that race in a color context is no longer an issue, but more sinister and much more effective is what I refer to as "cultural racism." The physical appearance of color no longer affects the national mindset, but the cultural background of those very same people can be problematic. This attitude harkens back to one of the most rudimentary principles of the colonizer mentality Fanon and Memmi identified long ago; denounce all elements of cultural identity of the colonized, thus forcing them to divest themselves of all opposition to the rule of the culturally superior colonizer society. If the colonized are to survive in the dominant culture they must accept the practices and beliefs of the latter and rid themselves of the vestiges of the exhausted, lifeless society of their ancestors: "leave your culture at the border" syndrome, we accept people of color so long as they don't rub their culture in our face.[9]

In 2008, to that political and social moderates making a decision on who they wanted to run this country Barack Obama carried none of the cultural baggage of "Blackness" that would have made it difficult to elect him; good-looking, articulate, educated, athletic, sharp-dresser, married with two beautiful daughters; Obama was everything White America recognized and understood as theirs. While he did have urban roots, he chose to raise himself above all that through education. No "bling" on this Black man; when he wore his favorite baseball team's hat the brim faced the front; no cornrow hair, tidy afro, cut short to the scalp; he did not wear oversize denim jeans, his slacks were tailored and pressed. This was not Dr. Dre, P. Diddy, Jay-Z, nor even Chris Rock, Black men who flaunted their "Blackness:" and wealth, for that matter. These are extremely successful individuals who openly identify with Black culture, whether that expression comes through music or comedy. These are the Black men Middle America is *not* ready to elect president; yet, the inferred perception remains unnoticed, race is irrelevant.

Recently, Congress, with the strong disapproval of a majority of Americans, narrowly, along strong partisan lines, passed the Healthcare Reform Bill (2010). The public criticism made all types of cases concerning length of the bill itself, government intrusion, and, of course cost, both socially and personally. The naysayers made their points and counterpoints, logical or illogical; they wrote their congressmen, or had tea parties with their friends to let Congress know firsthand of their displeasure; they exhausted the tools legally available to them to express their view, but missing in their rationalization was the question of race. That a majority of those Americans still lacking health coverage are people of color has never been mentioned. Yes, Congress did ensure that "illegal aliens" could not exploit the program, but like reduced spending on public education in California, how much of the public apathy to support assistance for this group have to do with presupposed assumptions that the benefactors of the program are of color?

After all has been written and said, the key purpose of this monograph has been twofold. Foremost has been in explaining the use of "Indian" imagery throughout American history as political and social metaphor. The image of "Indian" has therefore become the ideological property of American society, used and misused according to the whims of existing social or political needs coinciding with the nation's shared colonizer psychosis and the need to somehow rationalize away the extermination and exploitation of Natives. The end result is a concept of "Indian" passed down from generation to generation imbued with all the qualities of "inferior" entity, thus justifying their marginalized existence in American society. During the past half-century film and television have acted as conduits to sustain these beliefs through the White (sub)Conscience, a subliminal acceptance of White supremacy, stripped of the hateful language, instead Hollywood scripts, following the social and political movements of the time, gave the "Baby-Boomer" generation an Indian-ness ideologically still linked to the demeaning "Indian" of the colonizer mentality America of the eighteenth and nineteenth centuries very much enveloped in racist thought.

Consequently the second significant goal has been to expose the existence of this hateful and exploitative anachronism within contemporary thought. The White (sub)Conscience has given Americans the ideological Kevlar to deflect any projectiles carrying accusations of racism. As the generations of Americans exposed to the national image of "Indian" through film and television mature their descendants have inherited the concepts of Indian-ness each and every generation of Americans held before them through the continuing exposure of these films and series without placing the "Indian" in a proper racial or social context. It requires too much work to explain to novice viewers of these programs that while the story is entertaining the "Indian" depictions are flawed.

Too many years of not understanding, or even caring, that the depictions of "Indians" and other people of color through popular culture are hurtful and degrading contributes to the ethical malaise society is guilty of in making the necessary changes in its thinking. The White (sub)Conscience is an addictive sedative impeding the national conscience from acknowledging a moral responsibility to seek a fair and race(cultural) sensitive solution to the significant social and economic inequalities people of color have been forced to endure in their role as cogs in America's capitalist steamroller.

A few years back I used an early version of this theme in a lecture to my colleagues in the history department as part of a staff development assignment. At the end of the presentation one of my former colleagues stood up angrily and accused me of calling him a racist. Before I had the opportunity to answer him another person intervened to diffuse the situation. He never brought up the subject again and I was not about to broach the issue to him. Had we spoken I would have explained that the accusatory element of the White (sub)Conscience must be recognized at a cultural and social level, not as an individual. It is the society that has the race problem; the individual merely adopts the views and beliefs the mainstream community has come to value.

Three hundred years of racist ideology can not be erased by a simple piece of legislation, the comfort subliminal racism provides is too alluring. Humans are resistant to change; when confronted with decisions forcing them to alter their way of life defiance to chance is inevitable. The White (sub)Conscience gives the impression of progressive racial attitudes without the personal sacrifice needed to make those advancements really occur. All the answers to convince themselves they are doing the right thing are present in the logic, but it merely masks the reality of what does not get fixed: because there is no problem. There have been superficial race advancements in the United States, but the deepest problems confronting this nation continue to go unresolved.

As I try to understand our failure to acknowledge our delusion on race, I consider the analogy of an individual who is seriously ill and recognizes some of the symptoms associated with his/her malady, however they refuse to seek medical help because to visit the doctor is to admit one is sick. The longer the person avoids medical attention the more serious the illness gets, but fearing the bad news the doctor will give them, and the long and painful treatment ahead, is more disturbing than the acutely painful sensation the sickness is causing. If not treated properly the disease can be life-threatening, but denial is more appealing than the cure; the sickness remains hidden and the corrosive consequences go untreated.

Can the malady still be cured? I have too much faith in the human spirit to believe otherwise. Do I have the answer? Unlike the pundits of FOX-NEWS, I am not so pretentious to believe I have all the answers to rescue humanity, or at least the "Right Americans" of the United States. I am merely the purveyor of an ideology of denial. A philosophy that has prevented this nation from fully exploiting the diverse nature of "exotic" cultures it currently has at its disposal, due to the negative value context the ideology subliminally radiates. The White (sub)Conscience is nothing more than a theory, a way at looking at how society views race. It is meant to explain how the rationalizations and fears associated with the subliminal guilt of a colonizer society from an earlier America can still thrive in today's world. It was a place where dark-skinned people threatened the existence of God-fearing, hard-working, honest Whites seeking merely to raise their families. But, more importantly it was a space that flourished within the psyche of a people unable to morally explain their exploitation and abuse of indigenous peoples and people of color in the nation's formative years. Recently, a White woman, appearing to be in her late-sixties, early-seventies, attending a Tea Party protest, apparently distraught at the current state of social and political affairs in the United States., lamented, "This is not the America I grew up in!" No, it isn't...or, is it?

EPILOGOUE NOTES

[1] My son's name actually comes from his mother's middle name, Danette, not the Fess Parker television character.

[2] Interesting enough, there were many Black characters during the series, but I can recall only one instance when the individuals were referred to as anything other than Black. This is significant because we are talking about late-eighteenth century Kentucky, slave culture and all of its accoutrements. Culturally sensitive to the era *Boone*'s Blacks were referred to by the "Black Power" identity more popular with young and urban African Americans. Incidentally, the one time "Black" was not used a slave catcher angrily called Gabe Cooper "Nigger," needless to say Cooper's response was quick and powerful and the man never made the mistake of using the term again.

[3] Grier, at 6' 5" 284 lbs, played profession football for the New York Giants from 1955-1962 and later the Los Angeles Rams from 1963-1967 as a member of the famed "Fearsome Foursome." Needless to say, Mr. Grier was an imposing figure.

[4] One critic pointed out that it was regular occurrence to have Parker blow up a bridge during the Revolutionary War one week and then help break up Aaron Burr's 1805 coup attempt.

[5] Interestingly, *Hadji*, used as a Muslim term of respect identifying an individual who has completed a pilgrimage to the holy city of Mecca, has taken on a whole new meaning to contemporary U.S. military forces in the Persian Gulf. *Hadji* is used as a derogatory and racist term for Arabs that some believe came from the 1964 series *Jonny Quest*, released in 2004 on DVD,

and the 1996 *The Real Adventures of Jonny Quest* series employing the same characters from the original series in updated stories, introducing the exotic character to a generation of viewers who soon would need a racial epithet to use against a new "other."

[6] During the 1852 election the Know Nothing Party supported a political plank implementing restrictions on immigration, especially against Germans, but the party was soundly defeated and forced to rethink its anti-immigration policy as it was resurrected into the Republican Party in the mid 1850s. The country was not ideologically ready to restrict immigration.

[7] Repealed in 1943; the State Department thought it looked bad for the United States to have a ban on immigration for a country who was an ally in the war against Japan.

[8] NSC 68: United State Objectives and Programs for National Security (April 14, 1950).

[9] Of course, except on festive holidays and at ethnic restaurants.

Bibliography

Books

Ambler, Marjane, *Breaking the Iron Bonds: Indian Control of Energy Development*, Lawrence: University of Kansas Press, 1990.

Appy, Christian G., editor, *Cold War Constructions: The Political Culture of United States Imperialism, 1945-1966*, Amherst: University of Massachusetts Press, 2000.

Ball, Eve, *Indeh: An Apache Odyssey*, Norman: University of Oklahoma Press, 1988.

Barson, Michael and Steven Heller, *Red Scared: The Commie Menace in Propaganda and Popular Culture*, San Francisco: Chronicle Books, 2001.

Bataille, Gretchen M. and Charles L. P. Silet, editors, *The Pretend Indian: Images of Native Americans in the Movies*, Ames: Iowa State University Press, 1980.

Bernardi, Daniel, editor, *The Birth of Whiteness: Race and the Emergence of U.S. Cinema*, New Brunswick, New Jersey: Rutgers University Press, 1996.

Biolsi, Thomas, *Organizing the Lakota: The Political Economy of the New Deal on thePine Ridge and Rosebud Reservations*, Tucson: The University of Arizona Press, 1998.

Bird, S. Elizabeth, editor, *Dressing in Feathers: The Construction of the Indian in American Popular Culture*, Boulder, Colorado: Westview Press, 1996.

Biskind, Peter, *Seeing is Believing: How Hollywood Taught Us to Stop Worrying and Love the Fifties*, New York: Pantheon Books, 1983.

226

Bolt, Christine, *American Indian Policy and American Reform: Case Studies of the Campaign to Assimilate the American Indians*, London: Allen & Unwin, 1987.

Bordewich, Fergus M., *Killing the White Man's Indian: Reinventing Native Americans at the End of the Twentieth Century*, New York: Anchor Books Doubleday, 1996.

Berkhofer, Robert F., Jr., *The White Man's Indian: Images of the American Indian From Columbus to the Present*, New York: Vintage Books, 1978.

Cadwalader, Sandra L. and Vine Deloria, Jr., editors, *The Aggressions of Civilization: Federal Indian Police the 1880s*, Philadelphia: Temple University Press, 1984.

Carnoy, Martin, *Education as Cultural Imperialism*, New York: David McKay Company, Inc., 1974.

_____, *Faded Dreams: The Politics and Economics of Race in America*, Cambridge: Cambridge University Press, 1994.

Chinweizu, *The West and the Rest of Us: White Predators. Black Slavers and the African Elite*, New York: Vintage Books, 1975.

Churchill, Ward, *Struggle for the Land: Indigenous Resistance to Genocide, Ecocide and Expropriation in Contemporary North America*, Monroe, Maine: Common Courage Press, 1993.

_____, *Indians Are Us?* Monroe, Maine: Common Courage Press, 1994.

_____, *Fantasies of the Master Race: Literature, Cinema and the Colonization of American Indians*, San Francisco: City Lights, 1998.

Deloria, Philip J., *Playing Indian*, New Haven, Connecticut: Yale University Press, 1998.

Deloria, Vine, Jr. *Behind the Trail of Broken Treaties: An Indian Declaration of Independence*, Austin: University of Texas Press, 1974.

Deloria, Vine, Jr., and Clifford Lytle, *The Nations Within: The Past and Future of American Indian Sovereignty*, New York: Pantheon Books, 1984.

Dippie, Brian W., *The Vanishing American: White Attitudes and U.S. Indian Policy*, Middletown, Connecticut, Wesleyan University Press, 1982.

Drinnon, Richard, *Facing West: The Metaphysics of Indian Hating & Empire Building*, New York: Schocken Books, 1980.

Englehardt, Tom, *The End of Victory Culture: Cold War and the Disillusioning of a Generation*, Amherst: University of Massachusetts Press, 1995.

Foner, Eric, *Reconstruction: America's Unfinished Revolution, 1863-1877*, New York: Harper & Row Publishers, 1988.

Fanon, Frantz, *Black Skin, White Masks*, New York: Grove Press, 1967 (c1952).

_____, *The Wretched of the Earth*, New York: Grove Press, 1963, (c1961).

FitzGerald, Frances, *Fire in the Lake: The Vietnamese and the Americans in Vietnam*, New York: Vintage Books, 1972.

Friar, Ralph E. and Natasha A. Friar, *The Only Good Indian: The Hollywood Gospel*, New York: Drama Book Specialists, 1972.

Gibson, James William, *Warrior Dreams: Violence and Manhood in Post-Vietnam America*, New York: Hill & Wang, 1994.

Gladwin, Thomas and Ahmad Saidin, *Slaves of the White Myth: The Psychology of Neocolonialism*, Atlantic Highlands, New Jersey: Humanities Press, 1980.

Goldberg, David Theo, editor, *Anatomy of Racism*, Minneapolis: University of Minnesota Press, 1990.

_____, *Racial Subjects: Writing on Race in America*, New York: Routledge, 1997.

Gossett, Thomas F., *Race: The History of an Idea in America*, Dallas: Southern Methodist University Press, 1963.

Hilger, Michael, *The American Indian in Film*, Metuchen, New Jersey: Scarecrow Press, 1986.

_____, *From Savage to Nobleman: Images of Native Americans in Film*, Lanham, Maryland: Scarecrow Press, 1995.

Horsman, Reginald, *Race and Manifest Destiny: The Origins of American Racial Anglo-Saxonism*, Cambridge: Harvard University Press, 1981.

Hoxie, Frederick E., *A Final Promise The Campaign to Assimilate the Indians, 1880-1920*, Lincoln: University of Nebraska Press, 1984.

Huston, Althea C., et al, *Big World Small Screen: The Role of Television in American Society*, Lincoln: University of Nebraska Press, 1992.

Kelly, Lawrence C., *The Assault on Assimilation: John Collier and the Origins of Indian Policy Reform*, Albuquerque: University of New Mexico Press, 1983.

Kilpatrick, Jacquelyn, *Celluloid Indians: Native Americans and Film*, Lincoln: University of Nebraska Press, 1999.

Kugel, Rebecca, *To Be the Main Leaders of Our People: A History of Minnesota Ojibwe Politics, 1825-1898*, East Lansing: Michigan State University Press, 1998.

LaFeber, Walter, *America, Russia, and the Cold War, 1945-1996*, 8th edition, New York: The McGraw-Hill Companies, Inc., 1997.

May, Earnest R., editor, *American Cold War Strategy: Interpreting NSC 68*, Boston: Bedford Books, 1993.

Memmi, Albert, *The Colonizer and the Colonized*, New York: The Orion Press, 1965.

Miller, Stuart Creighton, *Benevolent Assimilation: The American Conquest of the Philippines, 1899-1903*, New Haven: Yale University Press, 1982.

Miller, Toby, et al, *Global Hollywood*, London: British Film Institute, 2001.

Nagel, Joane, *American Indian Ethnic Renewal: Red Power and the Resurgence of Identity and Culture*, New York: Oxford Press, 1996.

Nelson, Dana D., *The World in Black and White: Reading "Race" in American Literature 1638-1867*, New York: Oxford University Press, 1993.

O'Connor, John E., *The Hollywood Indian: Stereotypes of Native Americans in Film*, Trenton, New Jersey: New Jersey State Museum, 1980.

Owens, Louis, *Mixedblood Messages: Literature, Film, Family, Place*, Norman: University of Oklahoma Press, 1998.

Painter, Nell Irving, *Standing at Armageddon: The United States, 1877-1919*, New York: W.W. Norton & Company, 1987.

Philp, Kenneth R., *John Collier's Crusade for Indian Reform, 1920-1954*, Tucson: University of Arizona Press, 1977.

Prucha, Francis Paul, *The Great Father: The United States Government and the American Indians*, abridged edition, Lincoln: University of Nebraska Press, 1984.

Rollins, Peter C., editor, *Hollywood as Historian: American Film in a Cultural Context*, Lexington: University of Kentucky Press, 1983.

Rollins, Peter C. and John E. O'Connor, editors, *Hollywood's Indian: The Portrayal of the Native American in Film*, Lexington: University of Kentucky Press, 1998.

Root, Deborah, *Cannibal Culture: Art, Appropriation, and the Commodification of Difference*, Boulder, Colorado: Westview Press, 1996.

Rowe, John Carlos, *Literary Culture and U.S. Imperialism: From the Revolution to World War II*, Oxford: Oxford University Press, 2000.

Said, Edward, *Orientalism*, New York: Vintage Books, 1978.

Saxton, Alexander, *The Indispensable Enemy: Labor and the Anti-Chinese Movement in California*, Berkeley: University of California Press, 1971.

Scheckel, Susan, *The Insistence of the Indian: Race and Nationalism in Nineteenth-Century American Culture*, Princeton: Princeton University Press, 1998.

Sheehan, Bernard, *Seeds of Extinction: Jeffersonian Philanthropy and the American Indian*, New York: W.W. Norton & Co., 1973.

Singer, Beverly R., *Wiping the War Paint Off the Lens: Native American film and video*, Minneapolis: University of Minnesota Press, 2001.

Slotkin, Richard, *Regeneration Through Violence: The Mythology of the American Frontier, 1600-1860*, Middletown, Connecticut: Wesleyan University Press, 1973.

_____, *The Fatal Environment: The Myth of the Frontier in the Age of Industrialization, 1800-1890*, Middletown, Connecticut: Wesleyan University Press, 1985.

_____, *Gunfighter Nation: The Myth of the Frontier in Twentieth-Century America*, Norman: University of Oklahoma Press, 1988 (c1982).

Spence, Mark David, *Dispossessing the Wilderness: Indian Removal and the Making of the National Parks*, New York: Oxford Press, 1999.

Steadman, Raymond William, *Shadow of the Indian: Stereotypes in American Culture*, Norman: University of Oklahoma Press, 1982.

Stockel, H. Henrietta, *Survival of the Spirit: Chiricahua Apaches in Captivity*, Reno: University of Nevada Press, 1993.

Thomas, Nicholas, *Colonialism's Culture: Anthropology, Travel and Government*, Princeton: Princeton University Press, 1994.

Torres, Sasha, editor, *Living Color: Race and Television in the United States*, Durham, North Carolina: Duke University Press, 1998.

Trafzer, Clifford E., *As long As the Grass Shall Grow and Rivers Flow*, Fort Worth, Texas: Harcourt College Publishers, 2000.

Trouillot, Michel-Rolph, *Silencing the Past: Power and the Production of History*, Boston: Beacon Press, 1995.

Tucker, Frank H., *The White Conscience*, New York: Frederick Ungar Publishing Co., 1968.

Twaddle, Michael, *Imperialism: the State and the Third World*, London: British Academic Press, 1992.

Van Deburg, William L. *New Day in Babylon: The Black Power Movement and American Culture, 1965-1975*, Chicago: University of Chicago Press, 1995.

Vèa, Alfredo Jr., *La Maravilla*, New York: Plume, 1993.

Weston, Rubin Francis, *Racism in U.S. Imperialism: The Influence of Racial Assumptions on American Foreign Policy, 1893-1946*, Columbia: University of South Carolina Press, 1972.

Films

"Northwest Passage" (1939)

"Stagecoach" (1939)

"They Died With Their Boots On" (1941)

"Unconquered" (1947)

"Rio Grande" (1949)

"Across the Great Divide" (1950)

"Broken Arrow" (1950)

"The Last Outpost" (1951)

"The Savage" (1953)

"Arrowhead" (1953)

"Charge at Feather River" (1953)

"The Command" (1954)

"Drum Beat" (1954)

"Sitting Bull" (1954)

"Taza: Son of Cochise" (1954)

"Chief Crazy Horse" (1955)

"Dakota Incident" (1956)

"Walk the Proud Land" (1956)

"Pillars of the Sky" (1956)

"The Searchers" (1956)

"Trooper Hook" (1957)

"Tonka" (1958)

"Sergeant Rutledge" (1960)

"Geronimo" (1962)

"Cheyenne Autumn" (1964)

"A Man Called Horse" (1970)

"Little Big Man" (1970)

"Soldier Blue" (1970)

"Chato's Land" (1972)

"Jeremiah Johnson" (1972)

"Ulzana's Raid" (1972)

"Against a Crooked Sky" (1975)

"The Life and Times of Grizzly Adams" (1975)

"Winter Hawk" (1975)

"Grayeagle" (1978)

"Dances With Wolves" (1990)

"Gunsmoke: The Last Apache" (1990)

"Black Robe" (1991)

"Last of the Mohicans" (1992)

"Miracle in the Wilderness" (1992)

"Geronimo" (1993)

"Geronimo: An American Legend" (1993)

"Black Fox" (1995)

"Black Fox: The Price for Peace" (1995)

"Follow the River" (1995)

"Last of the Dogmen" (1995)

"Pocahontas" (1995)

"Tecumseh: The Last Warrior" (1995)

"The Indian in the Cupboard" (1995)

"Buffalo Soldiers" (1997)

"Smoke Signals" (2000)

"Doe Boy" (2001)

"Skins" (2002)

"The Missing" (2003)

Television
"Daniel Boone" (1964-1970)

"Jonny Quest" (1964)

Periodicals, Newspapers and the Web
Aliess, Angela, "The Vanishing American: Hollywood's Compromise to Indian Reform," *Journal of American Studies*, vol. 25 no. 3, 1991, December, pp 467-472.

Bovey, Seth, "Dances with Stereotypes: Western Films and the Myth of the Noble Red Man," *South Dakota Review*, vol. 31 no. 1, 1993, Spring, pp 115-122.

Churchill, Ward and Norbert and Mary Ann Hill, "Media Stereotyping and Native Response: An Historical Overview," Indian Historian 1978 11(4), pp 19-28.

Edgarton, Gary, "'A Breed Apart': Hollywood, Racial Stereotyping and the Promise of Revisionism in `Last of the Mohicans.'" *Journal of American Culture* v17 no. 2 (Summer 1994): 1 (20 pages).

"EID Finds that Church Rock Dam Break had little or No Effect on Residents," *Nuclear Fuel*, March 14, 1983.

Hilger, Michael, "Empathy Towards American Indians in Recent Films," Proceedings from the Native American Studies Conference at Lake Superior State University, October 16-17, pp 57-62.

Jojola, Ted, "Absurd Reality: Hollywood Goes to the Indians," *Film & History* 1993, 23 (1-4), pp 7-16.

Kennan, George, "The Sources of Soviet Conduct," *Foreign Affairs*, (July 1947), 566-82.

Leuthold, Steven M., "Native American Responses to the Western," (western films) *American Indian Culture and Research Journal* v 19 no. 1 (Winter, 1995): 153 (37 pages).

Mieder, Wolfgang, "The Only Good Indian is a Dead Indian, History and Meaning of a Proverbial Stereotype," *Journal of American Folklore* v 106, no. 419 (Winter, 1993): 38 (23 pages).

Pitman, Frank, "Navajos-UNC Settle Tailings Spill Lawsuit," *Nuclear Fuel*, April 22, 1985.

Prats, Armando Jose, "His Master's Voice(Over): Revisionist Ethos and Narrative Dependence from *Broken Arrow* (1950) to *Geronimo: An American Legend* (1993)," *ANQ: A Quarterly Journal of Short Articles Notes, and Reviews*, vol. 9 no. 3, 1996 Summer, pp 15-29.

Price, John A., "The Stereotyping of Native Americans in Motion Pictures," *Ethnohistory*, 1973 20(2), pp 153-171.

"Radiation: Dangerous to Pine Ridge Women," *Akwesasne Notes*, Vol. 12, No. 1, Spring 1980.

Shively, J. E., "Cowboys and Indians: Perceptions of Western Films Among American Indians and Anglos," *American Sociological Review*, 57: (6), Dec. 1992, pp 725-734.

Strong, Pauline Turner, "Animated Indians: Critique and Contradictions in Commodified Children's Culture," *Cultural Anthropology*, v 11 no. 3, (August, 1996): 405 (20 pages).

Telotte, J. P., "A Fate Worse Than Death: Racism, Transgression and Westerns," *Journal of Popular Film and Television*, Fall 1998, 26:3, pp 120-127.

Umland, Sam, "The Representation of the Native American in the Hollywood Western," *Platte Valley Review*, vol. 19 no. 1, Winter 1991, pp 49-70.

Weaver, Jace, "Ethnic Cleansing, Homestyle," *Wicazo Sa Review*, v 10 no. 1 (Spring 1994): 27 (13 pages).

Film Reviews and Criticisms
Baird, Robert, "'Going Indian': In and Around *Dances With Wolves,"* Michigan Academician*, v 25 no. 2, 1993 (Winter), pp 133-146.

Dozier, Lynne, *"Dances With Wolves:* Lessons from Loo Ten Tant's Journal," *English Journal*, v 83 no. 1 (January 1994): 34 (5 pages).

Edgarton, Gary and Kathy Merlock Jackson, "Redesigning Pocahontas: Disney, the "White Man's Indian," and the Marketing of Dreams," *Journal of Popular Film and Television*, v 24 not, (Summer 1996): 90 (9 pages).

Galloway, Margaret, "Native American Women and the Pocahontas Complex," *Journal of American Studies Association of Texas*, 1991, 22, pp 83-88.

HTTP://us.imdb.com/plot?0118790, *International Movie Data Base*, Film review.

James, Caryn, "Frugging with Wolves," *New York Times*, v 140, sec.2 (Sunday, January 13, 1991).

Kael, Pauline, "Dances With Wolves," *New Yorker* v 66 no. 44, (Dec. 17, 1990), 115 (2 pages).

Kasdan, Margo and Susan Tavernetti, "The Hollywood Indian In *Little Big Man:* A Revisionist View," *Film & History*, 1993, 23 (1-4), pp 70-89.

Manchel, Frank, "Cultural Confusion: *Broken Arrow:* A Look Back at Delmer Daves' *Broken Arrow,"* *Film & History* 1993, 23 (1-4), pp 57-69.

Ostwalt, Conrad, *"Dances With Wolves:* An American Heart of Darkness," Literature Film Quarterly*, v 24 no. 2 (April 1996): 209 (8 pages).

Romney, Jonathan, "The Last of the Mohicans," *New Statesman & Society* v 5 no. 227 (November 6, 1992), 41.

Sarf, W. M., "Oscar Eaten by Wolves," *Film Comment* XXVII/6, Nov-Dec 1991, pp 62-64 and 67-70.

Sterner, Alice P., "A Guide to the Discussion of the Technicolor Screen Version of *Northwest Passage*," *Photoplay Studies* 6, no. 9 (1940).

"The New York Times Film Reviews," New York: *New York Times,* December 1964.

Music Lyrics
"Courtesy of the Red, White and Blue (The Angry American)," lyrics by Toby Keith, (2003).

Made in the USA
Las Vegas, NV
04 March 2021